URBAN CHRISTIANITY
AND GLOBAL ORDER

URBAN CHRISTIANITY AND GLOBAL ORDER

THEOLOGICAL RESOURCES FOR AN URBAN FUTURE

A N D R E W   D A V E Y

HENDRICKSON PUBLISHERS

Urban Christianity and Global Order
© 2002 by Andrew Davey

Hendrickson Publishers, Inc.
P. O. Box 3473
Peabody, Massachusetts 01961–3473

The Hendrickson Publishers edition of *Urban Christianity and Global Order* is a slight revision of the SPCK edition and is published under agreement between Hendrickson Publishers, Inc., and the Society for Promoting Christian Knowledge.

Printed in the United States of America

First Printing—November 2002

First published in Great Britain in 2001 by
Society for Promoting Christian Knowledge
Holy Trinity Church
Marylebone Road
London NW1 4DU
Copyright © Andrew Davey 2001

Library of Congress Cataloging-in-Publication Data

Davey, Andrew.
    Urban Christianity and global order : theological
resources for an urban future / Andrew Davey.
        p. cm.
    Includes bibliographical references and index.
    ISBN 1-56563-715-1 (pbk. : alk. paper)
    1. City churches. 2. City missions. 3. Cities and towns—
Religious aspects—Christianity. 4. Globalization—
Religious aspects—Christianity. I. Title.
    BV637 .D38 2002
                                        2002012442

Contents

Foreword

Urban experience is certainly in your face! Wander into an urban environment, and it does not remain passive—it confronts us. Make our home in a poor urban district, bring our family with us, and it will overwhelm the senses, change our patterns of behavior, our expectations, our modes of relationship, and our notions of transcendence. If we stay long enough, we may begin not to notice the squalor, the noise, the addiction, and the fragmentation. If we do continue to notice them, we may find that the infectious apathy, born of generations of powerlessness, overcomes us. We will complain but do little. If we do widen our horizons, we will be shocked to see that not far away, urban structures support others in lifestyles of extravagant wealth, and we will become aware of just how complex is the interplay of urban wealth and poverty.

In this book, Andrew Davey reminds us that the city is not to be understood primarily as a geographical space or as a historical and cultural event but more as a nexus of complex human and structural relationships. In recent years we have been made to appreciate how much economic structural relationships are now driving the expansion and contractions of our urban areas, their international interrelationships just as much as their internal dynamics. And within this great complexity of forces and powers, a few are beneficiaries, but most turn out to be losers in the lottery of urban relationships.

The urban environment is perhaps humanity's most complex example of the dynamic of politics, cultures, power, history, and the commodification and classification of place. Furthermore, even if this dynamic were ever to be understood, we would be touching upon only a fraction of the modern and postmodern story of the city. For we are aware as never before of the way in which cities are interconnected across the globe. An economic tremor in the hi-tech city of Bangalore can send shockwaves through the electronic markets of Tokyo. Pictures of a riot in Seattle will be flashed by CNN to cities of the world, and within moments copycat initiatives are sprouting everywhere. Tensions in Jerusalem will have New York worried, and rivalries in Karachi will affect the polling booths of Bradford that same evening. The power of these strategic urban centers to affect the lives and well-being of millions cannot be underestimated, be it in the decomposing urban cores of the old world or the teeming shanties in and around the megacities of the globe. The needs, aspirations, and mindset of the cities will determine life for everyone, for whether we live in the cities or in the suburban sprawls or the rural villages, we are all urban now.

In all this mix of power, wealth, poverty, and powerlessness, the church is ever present, and usually at every level, breathing in much of the same atmosphere. In the face of the challenge, some congregations fearfully succumb to a defensive, inward-looking mode, while others adopt a brash mode of evangelistic superiority. But increasingly the church seeks to respond to its urban incarnation by becoming a listening and learning community. It learns to celebrate, to challenge, to build community, and to act prophetically; but above all it listens and it learns!

The church in the urban predicament has a long history of theological endeavor and Christian praxis from which to benefit. Many urban saints through the years have studied the situation and engaged with it. In all this we have had our urban heroes, heroines, and fools. In the latter half of the twentieth century there was an evident upsurge of activity and interest in urban mission. It has to be admitted, however, that sometimes we suffered from having more passion than analysis and understanding, and a great deal of charismatic urban activity turned out in retrospect to be ineffectual at a sustainable and deeper level. We were sometimes eaten alive by the powers that be, vastly underestimating the urban complexity by which we were confronted. It was a harsh and bitter learning experience—but we did learn. But the city does not go away. As the twenty-first century has dawned, so has an awareness of the growing influence of urbanization and its inextricable link with globalization. Governments the world over are seeking ways to regenerate the urban environment and ease social exclusion; megacities dominate the fears of the Two-Thirds World; the international trade in commodities, information, politics, and people are all being controlled from the cities; and the urban sprawls across the land and overwhelms the weaker rural cultures. We are all waking up to the stealth by which this has all been happening, and we begin to appreciate that the powers and principalities are alive and well and operating from a city near you.

As the world wakes up to urbanization and globalization and the extraordinary link that exists between the two, so many who want to understand today's city or today's world are engaging in urban studies and researching, learning, and discussing urban globalization. The church too begins to wake up to the challenge, for while the urbanologists have been shaping innovative disciplines of study and action, urban theology has grown and developed accordingly by leaps and bounds in this last decade. It has become a more informed and multidisciplinary activity.

In this book, Andrew Davey surveys this developing scene and offers those of us who want to play our part some frames of reference by which we might hope better to understand the complex web of factors that shape this urban environment in which we must live, work, and witness. His writing emanates from personal experience of living and working in poor urban communities and of traveling to many of the world's significant urban places to learn, listen, and engage with urbanologists and activists who are pushing at the frontiers of these disciplines. He has been very much involved in the development of the Anglican Communion's Urban Network, which is fostering vital partnerships with urban faith communities around the world, thereby seeking better to understand the dynamics of global urbanization so that we can work together to name the values that must underpin our local and global action in this urban world. Andrew Davey invites us to see the world and our urban communities with renewed insight and commitment. We live in exciting times!

Laurie Green
Bishop of Bradwell

Preface

This book is an attempt to explore how the thread of urban experience combines with one of the key threads of our time—globalization—and the implication that linkage has for the mission and life of the church. It is written as a primer—not the last word on its subjects—in the hope of introducing readers to some of the key commentators and approaches to urban trends at the beginning of the twenty-first century. This is not an attempt to offer an exhaustive survey of urban theory or theological responses to the urban experience but rather a reflection of some of the challenges and the opportunities of connecting theological and urban studies. By listening to the analysis, readers will begin to ask for themselves questions such as: how do we understand these glimpses of the urban process from a theological perspective; how will these forces shape the Christian community and its mission in the new millennium; and to what extent is the Christian presence in an urbanizing world the subject or object of those processes?

The responses that will emerge will reflect the context in which those questions have been asked. I hope that context will be centered on more than just one white male, employed as a national officer by the church, writing in London, but a reflection of the interactions that are possible as familiar and unfamiliar resources are identified and used to understand the future that is emerging. While this book is written with the contexts of Europe and North America in mind, I hope that it will be a resource for people attempting to make sense of their Christian discipleship in an urban world. If nothing else, the hope is that readers will look at their city and church in the midst of many changes, with new eyes.

While a review of the biblical engagement with the urban experience is offered, I have not attempted to continue that narrative through the Christian centuries. It is left to others to find new ways in which they might approach the urban theology of, say, Augustine, Isidore, Luther, Calvin, Maurice, Temple, Gutiérrez, and others less well known, in the light of key moments of urban change and the experience of Christians living as salt and leaven among and alongside those in the margins. Neither have I undertaken to provide a pastoral handbook for urban mission and ministry at the beginning of the twenty-first century, but again there are hints (for those who want them) concerning directions for urban pastoral praxis.

I would like to place on record my gratitude to those who have been drawn into this project in various ways, particularly Laurie Green and John Vincent, whose engagement with these issues in terms of writing and praxis has been vital in developing my praxis. Among those engaging intellectually with the impact of the urban I would like thank Bob Catterall, editor of *CITY*, and Doreen Massey of the Open University, for their interest, wisdom, and conversation on some of the key themes of this book. Colleagues in the Board for Social Responsibility and members of the Urban Bishops Panel have also been insightful and supportive from the earliest stages. I am grateful to Mike Mata of Claremont School of Theology, California; Brigitte Kahl of Union Theological Seminary, New York; and Tim Scott, who have all offered suggestions and comments on various parts of the text; as well as to Ruth McCurry of SPCK for picking up and running with this project. This book would not have been possible had it not been for the people of Peckham, the Elephant and Castle, and Lewisham, communities in south London where I have encountered a human aspect of globalization and urbanization in churches, on the streets and in many conversations. My love to Alison, Phoebe, and Isaac, who have lived with the project and provided space and a place called home to be human and loved.

Previous forms of some of this material have appeared in *Theology, The International Review of Mission, Crucible, CITY,* and *Liberation Theology UK;* other parts have been shared as papers with the Urban Theology Seminar at St. Deiniol's Library, Hawarden, 1999; the Claremont School of Theology Urban Convocation, fall 2000; and the 2001 meeting of the Episcopal Urban Caucus in New London, Connecticut. This edition is a revision of the text originally published in Britain by SPCK.

Part One

Understanding an Urbanizing, Globalizing World

Chapter One

Encountering the Urban

You only have to walk down the streets of any major city to encounter the world. Whether it is London, New York, Toronto, or Sydney you will quickly come upon the retailing and trading of different ethnic communities: many established for a number of generations, others recently set up. You will see goods displayed that have been made in the factories and sweatshops of the South; fruit and vegetables, some of which have traveled by air; financial institutions carrying the names of distant states; and meeting places labeled in numerous languages. Magazines and newspapers will combine the issues of communities thousands of miles away and those in the immediate locality. Posters and graffiti will advocate the political causes of regions on other continents. The experience of such a street scene can no longer be considered exotic. It is becoming the reality in numerous small towns and cities as well as those places previously thought of as cosmopolitan cities. The diverse ethnic cultures encountered will form part of the civic community—sending children to its schools, participating in local politics, paying local and national taxes, and calling on local medical and social services, just as numerous groups of immigrants have done before them.

The foreword to a recent history of London, for example, begins:

It is no accident that the story of London begins with "foreigners." There was no settlement at all on the banks of the Thames before the arrival of the Romans. Londoners owe their city, so to speak, to the Italians, and its whole development . . . is a tale of successive migration, wave upon wave of outsiders who have made their mark upon London, given it their own distinctive flavor, while at the same time becoming assimilated into the metropolitan melting pot. (Inwood 1998, xvii)

Roy Porter goes on to name the groups and individuals that have made London "one of the world's most cosmopolitan cities, a great experiment in a polyglot, multi-[ethnic] society" (Inwood 1998, xviii). The encounter with the global in urban places goes back hundreds of years. But just as the skyline of the city is changing, so too are the communities that live in its shadow. London's claim to be a world city is not based solely on its power and economic base. The city is a microcosm of the world, holding not just an ethnic diversity but an economic diversity where issues of justice and human rights must be tackled, where the mission of the church must be at the front line.

Walk further down an average street today and the realities of those connections and networks will become even more apparent, as new businesses, new ways of living and communicating come into view. Travel agents advertise cheaper and cheaper fares, making long-distance journeys a more frequent possibility. Telecommunication offices offer phone, fax, and e-mail rates that undercut those of mainstream service providers. Because of instant connections, people no longer wait weeks for that letter from home, and they no longer plan months for that visit. These new businesses allow an immediacy of communication at prices and speeds that few thought possible in past decades. Some of these businesses are fronted by religious bookshops offering publications on lifestyle, healing, and deliverance and artifacts for worship or festivals. Others offer training in information technology, legal, or business skills. Some even offer combinations such as Christian Business Schools or Islamic Resource Centers.

The contemporary city is a place where worlds meet. The diversity of the multicultural community stands in stark contrast to the mono-ethnic housing or industrial area on the city's fringe. But there too the dynamics of the urban and the global are active: in the perceptions of the residents regarding *their* city; in the ownership of nearby companies and the global forces they face; in the shoes to be found on the children's feet (or merely in their dreams); in the take-out food and in the satellite entertainment beamed to the local pub.

Wherever the street corner on which we stand, the city comes at us—changing, demanding, connecting, frustrating, excluding, embracing, conflicting. One leading urbanologist wrote of this "in your face" or rather "at your feet" experience: " 'Transform the World'—all well and good. It is being transformed. But into what? Here, at your feet, is one small but crucial mutation" (Lefebvre, quoted in Borden et al. 2001, 179).

The Urban Challenge

In the first decade of the twenty-first century our world will reach that symbolic point when over half of the global population will live in urban settlements: maybe a few years later than some had predicted, but it will be a period when the inhabitants of our planet pass a milestone at a speed that means few will notice it.

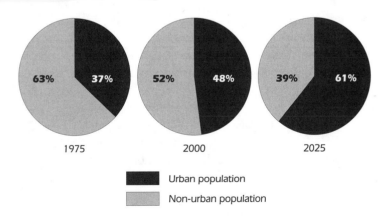

Figure 1.1: Global urban growth, 1975–2025.
Source: United Nations, 1996.

The towns and cities of previous generations are almost unrecognizable as new patterns of community, communication, work, and leisure shape the built environment. New settlements emerge—some highly planned, others seeming anarchic with little control over layout or purpose. In some places, as high-tech towers rise in the core zones, new areas of suburban residence, manufacture, and leisure sprawl at the edges; on the edge of other cities new impermanent settlements emerge because of the inability of authorities to accommodate or absorb those who are seeking a new home. Elsewhere there is decay or stagnation as old industries disappear, often transferring production to another continent, and housing no longer meets the demands of those for whom it was intended.

The urban population changes with social transition, migrancy, community tensions, and civil conflict. New demands are made on urban settlements to accommodate a vast array of groups and minorities within a common space: a process accompanied by competition and conflict as well as new forms of cooperation and coexistence. In an age of globalization, new forces are shaping settlements as new patterns of commerce and communication make many of the old foundations of settlements redundant. Employment becomes temporary and insecure; economic disparities become more apparent; migration makes many settlements transitional; the destiny of the urban area is often determined by corporations and market forces that are based on other continents.

The urban experience is increasingly common, presenting previously unanticipated challenges and opportunities. Although regions and cities are at various stages of the development or decline, the culture of the city is increasingly global, and this has far-reaching consequences even for the most rural societies.

Despite the infinite and intricate variations of tradition and culture which exist between nations, cities appear to have and to be acquiring more in common than they have differences. Urban places have many similarities of physical appearance, economic structure and social organization and are beset by the same problems of employment, housing, transport and environmental quality. (Clark 1996, 2)

Those who do not dwell in urban areas are similarly affected through the dominance of the urban in a society's life: through urban-based media and national institutions, through the flow of goods from migrants, and through the ever-increasing demands made on agricultural production by the urban populace.

A Challenge to the Church

The world is now an urban place. The resources and concerns of the church need to acknowledge this. This new situation means that, more than ever, theological reflection is needed on cities and the future of urban life. Some parts of the church have been engaged for many years with a wide range of initiatives that have raised questions about mission and ministry priorities. Engagement with government at all levels has taken place on vital issues of social justice, the environment, and the future of work. New patterns of church life and ministry have emerged in communities with few material resources where there has been little history of confident local leadership. The warranted concentration in the past on "urban priority areas" or areas of multiple deprivation has meant that many of the external factors that create those pockets of poverty and social exclusion have not been adequately addressed. A UK think-tank report commented: "Few policy makers have been clear about whether urban problems should be understood as problems fundamentally *of* cities or problems *in* cities" (Greenhalgh and Worpole 1997, 172). Philip Sheldrake expands this into theological language:

If there are sinful structures of exclusion and social deprivation these are not limited to particular districts within cities but affect, perhaps I should say "infect," the city as a whole both as built space and human community. . . . "Urban Priority Areas" are what they are, socially and economically, because of wider cultural failures concerning the nature of what it is to live publicly and the definition of human life as interdependence, the lack of a philosophy of humane environments, of community and the like. As a corporate expression of human self-definition, the city as a whole is a statement about the boundaries and potential of what it is to be human. (Sheldrake 2000, 166)

The theological challenges of the urban process today are those that have confronted Christians whenever the faith has been taken into unfamiliar patterns of social life. What are Christians called to be and do in a context so different from any which they have encountered before? What ministries and communities are Christians called to bring into being? In what ways can the human city be shaped to reflect the priorities and values of the kingdom of God? In the urban community, the simple question "Who is my neighbor?" demands a new answer.

Postcolonial migration brings the global to our doorstep. Bishop Theodore Eastman has written, "Everyone and everything is gathered in the city. . . . In a city one cannot separate those who are far off from those who are near. The exotic stranger from someplace else is a next door neighbor" (Eastman 1986, 228). The quintessential urban experience is the encounter with the stranger on an intimate as well as an immense scale. This will inevitably involve the meeting of cultures—the meeting of ethnic cultures from different parts of the planet, of rural and urban cultures, of the cultures of different streets or blocks that exist in proximity. That meeting is where negotiation begins—how, together, do we plan and shape the urban communities we want to live in, given a myriad of expectations, needs, and interests (see Sandercock 1998)? The face-to-face encounter is now complemented and complicated by the encounters made possible through information technology that links cities.

The brochure for the 1998 SCUPE Urban Congress in Chicago set the agenda thus:

To realize our calling in time for the new millennium, the urban church will need to raise up a new generation of leadership. It is time for those of us whose minds and imaginations have been captured by the city to think strategically about whom we disciple. Who is God calling to carry forward the work already begun? How should they be trained, and what do they have to teach their elders? How can we bridge the generation gaps? Who can cross the chasm of class differences? Who will be able to break down barriers between men and women, city and suburb, ethnicity and education and economic status? It is time to be intentional about raising up these leaders—the future of the city will be determined by a new generation of leadership.[1]

Looking for Tools

A commitment to engage with the reality of life in urban areas at the beginning of the twenty-first century demands a new set of tools for social analysis and for theological engagement. One has only to consider the rapid changes in the world of academic urban studies to realize the magnitude of the challenge; through the disciplines of geography, sociology, cultural studies, economics, architecture, and planning and in the vast array of media available, urban studies wrestles with the reality, the analysis, and interpretation of the urban experience. The scope and approach of urban studies enables it to begin, at least, to understand the dynamic, mutating, multilayered nature of our urbanizing, globalizing world. This approach is explained in the first volume of a key series from the Open University in Britain:[2] "The city cannot be thought of as having one geography and one history (and therefore one future). Instead cities are characterised by their new openness: to new possibilities, and to new interactions between people" (Massey, Allen, and Pile 1999, vii).

Gone are the great narratives of The City from Athens to Chicago, via Rome, Venice, and London. The destiny of Bombay and Singapore is not to become like Los Angeles. Neither are we dealing with a history of high civilization or democracy—the urban produces a myriad of cultural expressions and commodities, experienced in many different ways by rich and poor, included and excluded.

Instead, we must make sense of the networks, ideas, movements, and processes that we find shaping the urban world around us. Cities do not stand alone; urban populations are dynamic—the interaction between places is greater now than at any point in history. Issues of identity and belonging, living space and home are increasingly complex. This, then, is the context in which the Christian faith must be resourced in its mission, ministry, and theology. As we consider such questions and new approaches to the urban experience, the texts of our previous generation of urban theologians and practitioners may prove of limited value, whether they are Jacques Ellul, Harvey Cox, David Sheppard, or the Church of England's *Faith in the City* report. The challenge is to identify the strategies and resources that are needed if communities of Christian faith are to be salt, light, and leaven in the urban world.

The Task and Scope of Urban Theology

What is so significant about urban theological activity? What is the nature of this activity we call urban theology, and how might it contribute to the future of our urban areas?

Urban theology, or urban theological practice, comes from communities and individuals familiar with much of this from daily experience. Understanding this present, speaking of it, where the reality is sometimes denied, involves speaking from a context that is multilayered, interconnected, and globally connected in ways that urbanologists of even fifteen years ago could not conceive. As a contextual theology that is concerned with this reality of the world in which we live, those who are engaged with urban theological practice must reconceive its dynamics, its scope, and its constituency. Considering the task in the global context, Robert Schreiter suggests, "a task of any contextual theology is the negotiation of identity in a globalized world. That entails knowing something of the globalization process and its consequences for identity formation. It is on that basis that a critique of globalizaton can be mounted" (Schreiter 1997, 97).

Urban theology will straddle the global and local arising from the reflection and experience of people in real, concrete situations and analysis of all the forces that are shaping their community. If all theology, as a form of human production, is contextual, then almost all theology must be urban—coming out of those urban academic institutions, the university and seminary. But their context of activity is rarely acknowledged, and rarely does such activity attempt to change the setting in which it takes place.

Urban theology that is engaged and committed must be ✳ part of the movement that is associated with liberation theology as it takes as its subject, its defining concern, and draws its authority from the communities of the poor. That position must attest that it is orientated toward change, toward a different future for those who find themselves in poverty, excluded, or the victims of racism and violence. That different future cannot be a ghetto vision but must encompass the whole of the urban project, because that different future has implications for all who live in our cities and our urbanizing world.

Urban theology must, of its essence, be *praxis*-orientated, trenchant, impatient, observant, and engaged within the reality of life in all urban communities, as well as understanding the dysfunctional realities that produce areas of multiple deprivation. It must have a vision of how the future must be different and be committed to finding some of the mechanisms to make that a reality.

As the prophet said, "The philosophers have only interpreted the world in various ways; the point is to change it" (Marx 1976, 5). The scope of urban theology encompasses the concerns of an urbanizing world and the condition of the Christian presence and witness in it, rooted in struggles of the poor to shape and own their communities—whether it is the physical environment in which they live, the civil arrangements, or the *ekklesia* (the church) that they form around the Scriptures and the Eucharist.

Urban theology is a task that concerns and belongs in those communities. It is the process into which disciples bring their experience of their struggles so that, through the mutual activity of perceiving, reflecting, and engaging, an alternative future may emerge. Theology will inform all parts of praxis—that is the activity of engagement based on analysis and reflection.

Urban theology is not just the task of the theological specialist but the whole community as theologians. Those traditionally identified as theologians—priests, ministers, lay leaders—will find themselves drawn in to resource the community: informing the process of judgment, recording the process, reflecting and discerning alongside others.

South African theologian John De Gruchy describes the ordained minister as a practical theologian with the central tasks of discernment and leadership, enabling the community to ask and discovering with them, "What does God require of us here and now?" (De Gruchy 1987, 31). Answering this question implies a commitment to struggle and participation, with the minister becoming a resource for the local church. Urban theology is theology asking that question from a particular context/location—asking that question so the future may be different.

Answering that question will involve developing new capabilities and literacies within the church—understanding the forces and factors that shape the context, initiating conversations with others in similar contexts (maybe scriptural, maybe spatial), entering alliances with others who have an interest in that urban future (community groups, social movements, minority communities), opening dialogues with those who analyze cities and the urban experience (planners, sociologists, urbanologists, geographers, economists). Answering that question may result in a struggle with those who see the situation differently, who have a different answer. Urban theological practice and writing must involve a mutual, informed reading of the signs of the times. The communities that engage in these tasks will often have knowledge that supposed experts lack, experts who view that community as the object of their profession (see Sandercock 1998). Urban theological practice will involve engaging with those writing about the urban past, present, and future, as well as with reports and policy initiatives that emanate from government and think tanks. Faith communities will be shaped by the urban process, but they do have the potential to be protagonists in shaping the urban future and need the analytical and theological tools to take part in this role.

Notes

1. The Seminary Consortium on Urban Pastoral Education, based in Chicago. See website: www.scupe.com.
2. Details of the course "Understanding Cities" and accompanying resources can be found on the Open University website: www.open.ac.uk.

Chapter Two

Being Urban, Being Global

Thinking Urban

Thinking urban is a cultural transition that many are reluctant to undergo. As long ago as 1970 a sociologist wrote, "Britain is physically as urbanised as any nation in the world, yet as a society we seem to be extraordinarily reluctant to accept this fact" (Pahl 1970, 1). Despite the many social changes of the past thirty years, that reluctance is as evident today as it was in 1970. What is it that makes people so disinclined to acknowledge the urbanization they witness around them? Is it an inadequate vocabulary to express the processes they are part of? Is it a nostalgic fear of all things urban? What do cities and urban areas represent in the popular imagination that makes people so reluctant to understand themselves as part of an urban society? Recent official documents from the UK Government's Department for the Environment, Transport and the Regions consider the future of urban areas in England: Richard Rogers's Urban Task Force report *Towards an Urban Renaissance* (Rogers 1999) and *Our Towns and Cities: The Future,* an "Urban White Paper" (DETR 2000) considered anti-urban attitudes within British culture to be one of the obstacles to be overcome in their strategy for an "urban renaissance." Despite this, the same government department felt it necessary to placate the rural lobby by publishing a seemingly equivalent Rural White Paper of a comparative design and size, even though the nonurban population in England is below 20 percent. This may be accounted for by the fact that urban settlements only account for 7 percent of the nation's land use.

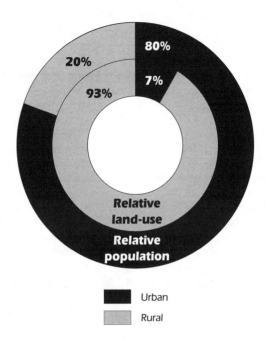

Figure 2.1: Population and land use in England.
Source: DETR 2000.

why is the church of England is reluntaut to urban?

This reluctance to embrace urbanism is particularly apparent within the Church of England, where the urban versus rural scenario is often played out as if the urban threatens the basic tenets of faith concerning the nature of the church. The urban church seems to represent the antithesis of the popular image of the church on the village green or the tranquility of the cathedral close. When Conservative Prime Minister John Major wanted an image of an ideal Britain he included warm beer and "matrons cycling to matins" past a village green laid out for the afternoon cricket match. Robert Orsi identifies similar attitudes when he comments:

> Nostalgia and dissatisfaction with the qualities of urban life in an industrial and then post-industrial society have created a lasting myth of small towns and family farms as the bedrock of all that is characteristically American. . . . (Orsi 1999, 13)

Faramelli, Rodman, and Scheibner spell out the implications for the Episcopal Church in the United States:

> the Episcopal Church has difficulty in calling a program "urban". Whether that resistance is a cultural bias or not is hard to determine. Certainly the many pockets of rural poverty must not be ignored. It is clear, however, that there are political problems in referring to a program as "urban", a legacy related to race and class, since the term *urban* to middle-class and white Episcopalians conjures up images of race and poverty. But the aversion to the word is probably also related to a deeply rooted distrust of cities that has been part of the American tradition since the days of Thomas Jefferson. (Faramelli, Rodman, and Scheibner 1996, 118)

The dilemma the church faces is how it can overcome such antipathy and false memory as it responds to some of the most acute challenges about the nature of human community that have ever been faced.

What Is "Urban"?

Defining the urban is the first problem. National statistics can be variable and inconsistent; comparative tables can be misleading. Some national statistics, such as Iceland's, will consider settlements with a population of a few hundred as urban; others will set various minimum levels: 1,500 (Ireland), 10,000 (Malaysia). Some add extra criteria: for example, the majority of inhabitants depending on nonagricultural activities, population densities of over four hundred per square kilometer, or the existence of a basic level of municipal government (see Clark 1996, 190–94). In the UK, over 90 percent of the population were considered to live in urban areas in 1991. The following criteria were used: "an urban area is defined as an area with land use which is irreversibly urban in character. Pre-requisites for inclusion of settlements are a continuous area of urban land extending for 20 hectares or more, and a minimum population of approximately 1,000 persons" (quoted in Rogers 1999, 29).[1] The US government Census Bureau offers a definition of "urbanized areas" as being the fully developed area of a city (which may have one or more "central places") and the adjacent built up areas (i.e., suburbs or "urban fringe") with a minimum population of 50,000. The Bureau defines an "urban cluster" as a densely settled territory that has at least 2,500 people but fewer than 50,000 people.[2]

Alongside urban population figures need to be set the comparative statistics of growth. While most European countries, the USA, and Canada reached a plateau just after World War II, many nations of the South are experiencing urban growth that changes the country's profile in less than a decade. The new types of growth are responded to in various ways, often depending on the state of the nation's economy. In the debt-ridden countries of Africa and Central America there is little public money to develop a new urban infrastructure, leading to informal settlements, overcrowding, and increasing pressure on scarce civic resources. A contrasting picture is provided by the development in some Southeast Asian cities where urban infrastructure is a highly technical part of an ongoing strategy for economic growth and competitiveness. Appearances may, however, be deceptive as questions of human rights and social justice, particularly for migrant communities, are often put to one side.

The growth of urban areas has an impact on rural areas. Urban growth will mean depopulation elsewhere with accompanying shortages of skills and capital. The demise of the rural workforce is matched by greater demands on the production capabilities of agriculture to feed and satisfy the demands of the urban masses. The interdependence of the urban and rural is crucial to our understanding of how communities of whatever size are sustainable in far more than just their ability to feed their people. The footprint of a city is the area affected by its existence. To its need for food must be added its demands for water and energy, as well as the polluting effect of its industries and transport. City footprints will often stretch well beyond national boundaries. It has been calculated that London's ecological footprint (that is, the environmental impact of seven million Londoners) is

125 times its surface area, and nearly equivalent to the total of Britain's productive land (Girardet 2000, 29); while Vancouver, Canada, is said to appropriate the productive output a land area nearly 200 times larger than its political area.

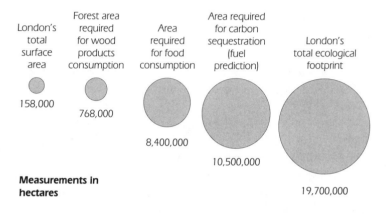

London's total surface area	Forest area required for wood products consumption	Area required for food consumption	Area required for carbon sequestration (fuel prediction)	London's total ecological footprint
158,000	768,000	8,400,000	10,500,000	19,700,000

Measurements in hectares

Figure 2.2: London's ecological footprint.
Source: Girardet 2000.

The extent of a footprint is global as, for example, resources are drawn from the rain forests of Southeast Asia, the copper mines of Africa, or the vineyards of Chile and Argentina, vast areas of plant life are required to consume the carbon dioxide output often in a different country, just as a city's pollutants may eventual fall as acid rain on the communities and forests hundreds of miles away. Wackernagel and Rees calculate that the hectare footprint per citizen is 4.27 in Canada, 5.1 in the US but only 0.38 in India (Wackernagel and Rees 1996, 86) This is, of course, assuming an average level of consumption; in reality the ecological footprint of the poorest 20 percent of the population in North America is less than a quarter that of the wealthiest 20 percent. A city's social, human, or economic footprint may be even greater—as decisions are made by governments and corporations with far-reaching effect, the cultural impact of urban lifestyles and attitudes proliferate, and patterns of demand and production vary according to the fashion and market forces. David Satterthwaite writes:

> It is difficult to estimate the scale of health risks faced by the workers and their families who make the goods which the consumers and enterprises within wealthy cities use. It is also difficult to adjust the calculations for a city's "ecological footprint" to take account of the goods and services that its enterprises produce for those living outside its boundaries. (Satterthwaite 1999, 92)

As we can see, the urban experience is not solely about statistics. Urban culture is endemic in our global society. The global powers of media and communications, of economics and politics, derive from cities, but there are few settlements where their impact is not felt. The cultural artifacts of the urban world move freely between city and village. Through advertising in all types of communication, the global brands of urban lifestyles captivate and create new cultures of consumption.

Neither is the urban process solely about the growth of cities. Even with the decline of the core areas of many cities in Europe and North America, the urban process continues as populations move out or change. Medium- and small-sized towns will grow in other parts of the country, and regional variations will emerge. In some regions the demand for housing will lead to acrimonious debates about where that housing will be placed—green field or brown field, using undeveloped land or reclaiming land from industrial or other use. Some cities will find their centers attracting new populations through deliberate policies, the evolution of cultural sectors, or commercial developments. This may include warehouse and loft conversions to residential accommodation, the expansion of higher education, or the promotion of an entertainment or club quarter. Such developments raise poignant questions about the alienation of residual pockets of older communities. (Gentrification often happens alongside areas

of social housing, which results in the city core being dominated by young single professionals and minority ethnic
communities.) Whatever happens, the urban process, the
urban experience, continues.

The denial referred to earlier is evident in the way that
the urban debate usually concentrates on areas of multiple
deprivation in need of regeneration. The suburban as well as
the exurban communities on the edges of cities must be included in thinking about our urban future. Although the
population of gated communities often do not think of themselves as part of the city, their employment and wealth are
no doubt bound up with the urban economy. (For an ex-
panded discussion of urban policy and social perception, see
Cochrane 2000.)

Defining the Processes

Tight definitions seem impossible, but as these terms will be
used regularly in this book, I will attempt to offer some indication of what might be meant.

Urbanization

Urbanization is the process through which urban settlements grow and develop. Urbanization may affect different
regions of a society at different speeds and in different
ways. People from rural areas are attracted to towns and
cities in search of work and social opportunity, often crossing national boundaries. In some regions cities expand rapidly, with little control being exercised over the planning of
new settlement areas and the provision of basic infrastructure needs. In other regions where the economy is booming,
urban growth is tightly controlled and planned, and city authorities eager to keep ahead in the information revolution
impose new patterns of urban life. Urbanization is not
an experience limited to developing countries and emergent economies. The situation in Britain, already described
where the population is on the move from the older indus-

trial cities of the north to London and the southeast, means urbanization—particularly in the form of suburban sprawl becoming a significant factor in the country's most populous region. In North America suburban sprawl has been a reality of urban living for more than half a century with its own segregated infrastructure of shopping strips, malls, and business parks planned with the assumption of massive automotive transport. Urban growth is not necessarily matched by the development of new communities of identity and belonging:

> Each year, we construct the equivalent of many cities, but the pieces don't add up to anything memorable or of lasting value. The result doesn't look like a place, it doesn't act like a place, and perhaps most significantly it doesn't feel like a place. Rather it feels like what it is: an uncoordinated agglomeration of standardized single-use zones with little pedestrian life and even less civic identification, connected only by an overtaxed network of roadways. (Duany, Plater-Zyberk, and Speck 2000, 12)

There is much happening within the phenomenon we choose to label "urbanization." Geographer David Harvey contends that urbanization is a process of production through which places become cities and towns—human settlements marked out, formally or informally, by the structures and streets, institutions, power structures in which that community lives and by which it organizes itself. Urbanization produces, sustains, and dissolves those arrangements in ever-changing configurations.

> Understanding urbanization is integral to understanding political–economic, social, and cultural processes and problems. But this is true only if we consider urbanization as a process (or more accurately, a multiplicity of processes) producing a distinctive mix of spatialized permanences in relation to each other. The idea that a thing called the city has casual powers in relation to social life is untenable. Yet the material embeddedness of spatial structures created in the course of urbanization are in persistent tension with the fluidity of social processes such as capital accumulation and social reproduction. (Harvey 1996, 419)

Urbanism

Urbanism is the cultural impact of the urban. The culture of the city is often hybrid, fusing a multiplicity of cultural forms, values, and lifestyles. Urban culture impacts on all communities. Government, commercial, and economic interests, the media, and so on are all urban based and orientate their policies, production, or output to the urban population, that is, the part of the population that is numerically greater or that has the greater spending power. The artifacts of everyday life are the carriers of an urban-based global culture. In Africa, Asia, and Latin America material resources (refrigerators, computers, televisions) flow back to rural areas from migrant relations who have settled elsewhere. Some of those items will be the channels through which urban-based media bring about significant cultural change as patterns of social, economic, and community life are questioned and urban lifestyles with their assumptions become acceptable. That urban-based media will also be the entry point for global influences.

Urban Process and Experience

Urban settlements are never static; there is constant change, whether it is growth or decay, regeneration or desertion. Sociologists of a previous generation talked of an urban cycle of growth and decline. More recent studies put the emphasis on the multilayered nature of urban life where contradictory processes may often be happening simultaneously in the same space. Urban space is contested, negotiated, and expropriated by its different social groups, its minorities, and new arrivals. Spatial questions arise of out of proximity, as the perceptions and expectations of the urban populace overlay each other or clash. In some places this can lead to the division of cities as a result of violent civil conflict (see Safier 1996). The intensity and speed of urban life offers possibility and potential that many are looking for, while others are bemused by the change in which they find themselves caught up.

The powers that compete for control of the city are not just its rich and poor or opposing political parties but multinational interests, often based in other cities in a different hemisphere. With the new connections, the flow of information and resources is accelerating at unprecedented levels, accompanied by economic interests and ideologies contending to shape a future that is urban and global. The urban experience is identified as critical in the development of scientific and cultural life. *Civitas,* from which we derive *civilization,* is about how the urban community is ordered for the benefit of its citizens. The *civitas* we seek in the new millennium is about how an urban people learn to live and organize together and handle that attribute of urban living that provokes change, creativity, and experiment—in patterns of social life, politics, and economics as well as the arts and science. This must also be where the urban experience raises profound questions of social justice and power— in what ways is living in an urban community convivial and sustainable for all?

Globalization

Globalization is an amalgamation of the most significant forces shaping our urban areas and our world today: a transition far from complete but impacting in unprecedented ways through numerous social, economic, political projects and practices. (Some would trace globalization back to earlier forms of global activity from the late Middle Ages: the opening up of trade routes between the old and the new worlds and the development of financial and trading institutions by Venetians and Germans; through later forms of colonialism and the development of transport and communication technologies.)

Changes in technology and economics have broken down the barriers of time and space, allowing instant interaction and "the dematerialization of space and distance." Revolutions in communications and travel lead to an explosion of information flowing between communities. The deregulation of finance has been succeeded by global economic systems expansion as corporations take on new forms of production and distribution. Companies will have interests in a number of places, and different parts of a production operation can be spread across locations, often with the ability to withdraw when profitability is threatened. Simultaneous to this diffusion of operations has been the concentration of capital in the control of multinational and transnational corporations, many of which have greater annual revenues than the gross domestic product of whole nations. For example, in 1998 IBM had a total revenue of $78.5 billion, greater than the GDP of the Czech Republic ($54.9 billion), New Zealand ($65 billion), or Egypt ($75.5 billion) (Thompson 2000, 105). If in 2000 retailers Wal-Mart had been classified as a country their $165 billion annual revenue would have placed them twenty-fourth in a ranking of countries' GDP (Chung, et al. 2001, 68).

At the other extreme, on a personal level globalization has changed things for the individual. Electronic banking, credit cards, and the Internet allow access to goods and services regardless of location in an instant (though the involvement of more traditional methods of delivery often remains unacknowledged); lower costs and easy access to travel and communications have altered the way in which people relate to foreign places, whether they are refugees, business people, or tourists.

The dynamics of interconnectedness mean that globalizing processes can be seen behind a growing global consciousness—people are aware of floods and disasters on the other side of the world almost instantly—as well as more virulent processes leading to a uniform, synthetic culture in the music, fashions, and consumer goods demanded by the young.

Health also needs to be understood in global terms, whether it is a new strain of flu or the rapid spread of HIV and AIDS, passed on quickly through the greater mobility of infected people; or smoking-related diseases spread through the commercial practices that have switched aggressive marketing from continents where smoking is actively campaigned against by governments, to places where there are fewer controls.

The global economy is organized in and through cities, as node points in vast interconnecting networks and systems that are oblivious to national boundaries or their impact on significant numbers of people who are excluded from the dividends of the new markets and opportunities that are emerging. The flows and processes of globalization are far from even in the access they create or their impact upon the global population. Doreen Massey writes on the uneven access to the new global mobility:

> different social groups, and different individuals, are placed in very distinct ways in relation to these flows. This point concerns not merely the issue of who moves and who doesn't . . . it is also about power in relation *to* the flows and the movement. Different social groups have distinct relationships to this anyway differentiated mobility: some people are more in charge of it than others; some initiate flows and movements, others don't; some are more on the receiving end of it than others; some are effectively imprisoned by it. (Massey 1994, 149)

(In the next chapter I will explore a particular analysis of how the global mobility of some poor groups is impacting on world cities.) As new experiences of exclusion emerge, globalization poses questions of social justice, identity, and belonging in new settings.

> [When] we encounter social exclusion, that is the inability to participate fully in the social life of a society, it will not just be about poverty, those who are left out financially, but also about those unable to access the connectivity, the conviviality of the global city. This impact in terms of employment/employability; in terms of commerce—the ability to access certain patterns of financial transaction; even one's ability to operate in the civic sphere, as electronic voting or electronic information services become the norm. Deprivation may need to be redefined in terms of capability to access certain levels of local and global networks. (Davey 1999, 383; see also Buffoni 1997)

The global dimensions of poverty led Anthony Giddens to
write:

> underclasses are not just pockets of deprivation within national
> societies, they are fault lines along which the Third World rubs
> up against the first. The social isolation which separates under-
> privileged groups from the rest of the social order within nations
> mirrors the division of rich and poor on a global scale—and is
> casually bound up with that division. First world poverty cannot
> be approached as though it had no connections with inequalities
> of a much broader scale. (Giddens 1994, 148)

Delocalization and Globalization

So what is the impact of globalization on the urban community? Two processes seem to come into play: *delocalization*
(Gray 1999, 57) and *globalization* (Robertson 1992, 173–74).
The first uproots activities and relationships from a sense of
place, displacing those that might be considered local into new
arrangements that are distant or global. For example, ticket-
ing for a national airline in the US or the UK can now take
place in India; a local telephone call to a firm may be rerouted
to an answering center on another continent. While it is often
assumed that globalization tends toward homogeneity, it is
actually stimulated by local or regional differences such as
skill base, wages, political stability, financial concessions, or
infrastructure. These attract as well as repel investment; the
nature of that investment and the goods or services that are
produced mean that a pair of socks can be produced identi-
cally in Ireland or India. The locality of production will depend on the local costs the producer is likely to incur. "There
would not be profits to be made by manufacturing worldwide
if conditions were similar everywhere. Global markets thrive
on differences between economies" (Gray 1999, 58).

    Globalization can be understood as a reassertion of the
local within the globalization process. While production tends
toward *delocalization,* markets are *global* and products may
need to be adapted to local conditions, be they cultural, cli-
matic, or whatever. The Japanese word for this business
strategy is *dochakuka*—an electronic product may need ad-
aptation if it is to impact a local market. Globalization can

also involve the rediscovery of identity or local significance in a global context. This may be an inherited or a new aspect of the local—a community's received custom or its new multicultural identity. In an urban community, globalization may take effect when the local built environment is under threat; a high street or marketplace considered by a global conglomerate to be "an investment opportunity" and ripe for redevelopment may have a local significance for which the community is willing to fight.

The delocalization of capital can remove the ability and willingness of businesses to engage in the local communities where their profits are made. This is particularly apparent in corporate philanthropy. For example, even in cities as significant as London, New York, or Tokyo, financial activity will be in the control of a range of companies, mostly transnationally owned, which have little engagement or interest in the institutions of the public infrastructure—schools, hospitals, libraries—preferring rather to contribute to more internationally significant educational or cultural institutions (business schools, opera companies) without a geographical association to the place of business (Sennett 2000).

The processes and phenomena examined in this chapter are unprecedented challenges within and between urban communities across the global stage. Neighborhoods of the mind and economy no longer end at main roads or rivers or center on the pub or corner shop, yet people still physically inhabit the urban built environment and interact with it. As we move between local and global neighborhoods we find ourselves interacting with new movements, new ways of thinking and understanding the human condition. In the next chapters I want to begin to explore this new landscape with some of the key guides who are writing about globalization and urbanization today.

Notes

1. The Urban Task Force used a minimum population figure of 10,000; this is followed by the Urban White Paper (DETR 2000).

2. For more information see the Census Bureau website: www.census.gov/geo/www/ua/ua_2k.html.

Chapter Three

Urban Sites and Global Places

Grasping the Global

Globalization has been, is, and will continue reshaping our world at an unprecedented speed. There is no denying the changes that we witness on our streets, through our computer networks, and in our pockets, as we carry around the paraphernalia of globalization—credit cards, mobile phones, plane tickets.

How we view globalization depends on the filters we have available. Like the current governments in Britain and the US, we may view globalization's intimate relationship with economic liberalism as inevitable—and believe we need to be toughening ourselves for competition in this brave new world. This can mean developing favorable relationships with key corporations, creating physical infrastructure, and looking to maximize the skills base in the information technology sector. Such acceptance has implications not just for how governments develop their domestic, social, and economic policies but also for how they engage with the global South, particularly those places on the periphery of the information revolution.

The global dimension of the contemporary city sets new challenges as new technologies and communications create unprecedented patterns of social life. This is true not just for the business world and the affluent but also for the poor, particularly for minorities whose communities now stretch beyond limited geographical ghettos, "groups who are doing a lot of physical moving who are not 'in charge' of the process in the same way" (Massey 1994, 149). As we have already noted, our engagement with poverty on a global stage must be informed by knowledge of the impact of globalization on the communities who live, quite literally, in the shadows of our booming economic institutions—often the poorest and least connected communities in the richest and most connected world cities.

In the next two chapters I want to explore the analysis and concepts offered by some of the key commentators on the new globalized urban context; from there I hope to begin to discern some of the ways in which the church might engage with the issues facing cities at the beginning of the third millennium.

Saskia Sassen: The Global City as Strategic Site

Urbanologist Saskia Sassen describes cities as being strategic sites in a new geography of centrality and marginality, which reproduces many of the old inequalities in new clusters, with little regard for national frontiers or regional geography (2000a, 2000b). Globalization binds cities in new hierarchies according to the intensity of the transactions that pass between them. The most powerful of these are the international financial and business centers—including New York, London, Tokyo, Paris, Frankfurt, Zurich, Los Angeles, Sydney, and Hong Kong. Another level is emerging, as the capacity and capability of cities in the global South is developed. This level includes cities such as São Paulo, Buenos Aires, Bombay, Bangkok, Taipei, and Mexico City. On this level Sassen comments, "there has been a sharpening inequality in the concentration of strategic resources and activities between each of these cities and others in the same country." She goes on to observe, "Alongside these new global and regional hierarchies of cities is a vast territory that has become increasingly peripheral, increasingly excluded from the major economic processes that fuel economic growth in the new global economy" (Sassen 2000a, 51).

For example, the cities of Africa do not feature in these hierarchies; technological and economic apartheid is apparent in the continued exclusion of continental Africa from the connectivity that is emerging (what Manuel Castells has called "the disinformation of Africa" [Castells 2000b, 95]). These hierarchies are dominated by national or regional capitals whose connectivity and infrastructure are usually light years ahead of other cities in their territory.

Sassen also detects "continuous border crossings" similar to flows and processes associated with global capital in another key grouping in the contemporary city—the new urban poor, a mobile migrant labor force upon which the infrastructure of the global city depends. The migratory poor in the global city are part of the unrelenting seepage through the cracked casings of the nation state (Sassen 2000a). Global changes allow the movement of people, not just money and information, across national frontiers in new flows.

> I think there are still representations of globality which have not been recognized as such or are contested representations. . . . What we still narrate in the language of immigration and ethnicity, I would argue is actually a series of processes having to do with the globalization of economic activity, of cultural activity, of identity formation. Too often immigration and ethnicity are constituted as otherness. Understanding them as a set of processes whereby global elements are *localized,* international labour markets are constituted, and cultures from all over the world are de- and reterritorialized, puts them there at the centre along with the internationalization of capital as a fundamental aspect of globalization. (Sassen 1998, xxxi)

Sassen envisages the claims that the poor, particularly women workers and migrant groups, make upon the city, becoming an increasingly significant part of the new transnational politics. This "signals a politics of contestation embedded in specific places but transnational in character" (Sassen 1998, xxxiv).

The global urban population changes with social transition, migrancy, and community tensions. New demands are made on urban settlements to accommodate a vast array of groups and minorities within a common space: a process accompanied by competition and conflict as well as new forms of cooperation and coexistence. In an age of globalization, new forces are shaping settlements as new patterns of commerce and communication make many of the old foundations of settlements redundant. Employment becomes temporary and insecure; economic disparities become more apparent; migration flows make many settlements transitional, as people come and go; the destiny of the urban area will be determined by corporations and market forces controlled by transnational interests. Centrality and marginality is a scenario played out at all levels. High-tech towers and executive residential buildings put core zones off limits to many citizens. Suburban gated communities similarly define social divisions in spatial terms. These social constructions are often found in other arenas—zoning and planning policy, immigration control, and welfare contraction. In other parts of the world, those cities struggling for a place in the new global hierarchies are hesitant about the status to be granted to impermanent settlements around which new arrivals flock. The city authorities seem unwilling or, more often in the face of readjustment programs, unable to afford to accommodate or absorb those who seek a new life and home.

Those who do not dwell in urban areas are similarly affected through the dominance of the urban in a society's life: the urban-based media and national institutions emphasize constantly the supremacy of the city. The ever-increasing demands made on agricultural production, water, and power by the urban populace reshape nonurban areas as subservient to the city's needs. Despite the city's dependency on these nonurban places and their produce, their significance is underestimated.

A key theme in Sassen's thinking is *valorization*—a socially embedded dynamic that sets criteria for valuing, for pricing economic activities, outcomes, or sites (Sassen 2000b, 60, 182). She writes of the *overvalorization* that happens around activities and places associated with the global financial markets and specialized service sectors. How this dynamic impacts on the hierarchy of cities has already been noted, but this can also be as evident in the prices associated with real estate in financial districts or associated residential areas, as it is with wages, thus introducing a very concrete spatial dimension into the equation (2000b, 41). This is paralleled by the *devalorization* of people, places, and activities associated with other parts of the economy, including many of those employed in the low-paid manual jobs or supplying the street-corner services on which the daily life of the global city depends.

> High prices and profit levels in the internationalized sector and its ancillary activities, such as top-of-the-line restaurants and hotels, have made it increasingly difficult for other sectors to compete for space and investments. Many of these other sectors have experienced considerable downgrading and/or displacement; for example neighbourhood shops tailored to local needs are replaced by upscale boutiques and restaurants catering to the new high-income urban elite. (Sassen 2000b, 60)

The forces that Sassen describes at work are restructuring cities and increasing the socioeconomic divisions within the wider urban context—the global city is the embodiment of the changes brought about by globalization. As the significance of certain cities and the activities they are based upon increases, a dysfunctionality enters the urban scene as the public and social infrastructure of the city is no longer sustainable. Teachers and some health professionals can no longer afford property prices, and a living wage is not paid to those upon whose services the urban economy depends—cleaners, security personnel, transport workers.[1] As the urban experience is increasingly common, the poor, driven to new patterns of migrancy by global economic changes, find themselves faring little better in highly developed urban centers, compared to the struggling cities and rural economies they have left.

> Global cities concentrate a disproportionate share of global corporate power and are one of the key sites for its valorization. But

they also concentrate a disproportionate share of the disadvantaged and are one of the key sites for their devalorization. . . . Both actors, increasingly transnational and in contestation, find in the city the strategic terrain of their operations. But it is hardly the terrain of a balanced playing field. (Sassen 1998, xxxiv)

The Church in the Global City

The church, as a noneconomic player, has been absent from much of Sassen's analysis, despite the deep religiosity apparent among the marginalized poor in the global city, as already described in London, and not least in the emergent Hispanic communities of the US. The church and other faith communities do have a "deeply embedded transnationalism" that continually crosses national borders and promotes significant global agendas—what other international nongovernmental body has the ability to mount a conscientization process like Jubilee 2000—the campaign which targeted international debt[2] (see Ottley 2000)? Alongside that transnationalism is the reality of the church's presence across the communities of the global city, penetrating even the citadels and gated communities of the new economy, though often it will find itself contending with distortions of faith in the belly of the beast.

There is much in Sassen's analysis which invites engagement with those concerned with economic and social justice. The rhetoric of valorization provides a significant tool for discussion of the processes that determine the distribution of wealth and resources on a global stage.

Bishop Laurie Green has commented on this:

we must take care not to be swept along with the rhetoric of globalization studies to accept that the economically significant world cities are the only centres of power. For although economics is a tremendously powerful factor on the world stage there are other forces which are equally important for a Christian analysis. (Green 2000, 16)

Why should some people, places, and activities be considered cheap while others are given value out of all proportion to reality? Why should the person sewing athletic shoes in Cambodia be paid or housed any differently from the person who sells them in New York—or for that matter the person who advertises them on MTV? Why is the stock trader sitting at the computer terminal more significant to the well-being of the corporation than those who maintain the office environment?

The city is contested, but what strategies will need to be pursued to make it a space of social and economic justice? On what criteria is human worth to be judged in the urban context? What form must the struggle for spatial justice take—who has a right to the space of the city? Who has a right to call the city home? What, and for whom, is the economy of the city? The struggle for justice must include the spatial dimension as a vital component; secure shelter is a vital contributor to human dignity, but with that must go a democratic right to participate in the shaping of community—its economy and its built environment.

Much of the scene Sassen describes is emergent or transitional; she writes of an emergent urban politics of contestation engendering new patterns of community life and a new politics of identity and culture among marginal groups. This is a scene that varies even within cities. It is a politics that breaks surface occasionally, in often gender-specific ways—through the persistence of women or the violence of men.

Maybe she is overoptimistic about the potential to reshape power in the global city. The "new cultural politics" that Sassen identifies has yet to make any real improvement in the lives of the majority of the poor of the global city (Zincone and Agnew 2000). Participatory citizenship can feel as remote from many residents of the global city as it was from the slaves and women of classical Athens. The potential of the movements that will lead those politics is a concern of our next commentator.

Manuel Castells: Informational Capitalism and the Shape of Resistance

A key figure in documenting these processes is the Spanish urbanologist, now teaching in California, Manuel Castells.

Anthony Giddens has compared his recent trilogy *The Information Age: Economy, Society, and Culture* (1997, 2000a, 2000b) with the seminal work of Max Weber. In his first volume, Castells traces a pattern of networked urban development, of globalization and the emergence of what he calls "informational capitalism." Information and its associated technology have become the vital determinants of the global economy at a time of economic and political restructuring. Global society is connected through networks— the exchange of information and processing of knowledge through flexible systems and organizational arrangements. These adapt, specialize, merge, and split with great fluidity. In commercial terms, "co-operation and networking offer the only possibility to share costs, and risks, as well as keep up with constantly renewed information. . . . Inside the networks, new possibilities are relentlessly created. Outside the networks, survival is increasingly difficult" (Castells 2000a, 187).

From an urban perspective, Castells writes of the role of the city in this new economy as a potential "space of flows." Restructuring has impacted the old industrial cities of Europe and North America; "the lower their position in the new informational network, the greater the difficulty of their transition from the industrial stage, and the more traditional will be their urban structure" (Castells 2000a, 433). He also highlights the emergence of new places based on technology and innovation, such as Silicon Valley in California (Castells 2000a, 64; see also Castells and Hall 1994). Globalization has led to the loss of the individual identity of cities, and this is nowhere more apparent than in the megacities, that is, cities of over ten million inhabitants, mainly situated in the global South. Castells questions the sustainability of these cities, which have the "distinctive feature of being globally connected and locally disconnected, physically and socially" (Castells 2000a, 436). "In a fundamental sense, the future of humankind, and of each mega city's country, is being played out in the evolution and management of these areas. Mega cities are the nodal points, and the power centers of the new spatial form/process of the information age: the space of flows" (Castells 2000a, 440).

In his second volume, Castells explores the reaction to the new informational world order. Alternative networks and social movements are reshaping and redefining their place in the new contexts with a remarkable dynamism. Through cultural action based on identity, gender politics, and innovative forms of community (ethnic, religious, and territorial) new patterns of network are emerging from below. These movements are determined to get away from enforced individualization of identity, centralized organization, and intervention. These social movements emerge because of global changes—the awareness of green issues, the demise of patriarchalism, political and economic changes, the new situations of the poor and migrants, and so on. They address specific or local issues, with the intention of reshaping or creating new spatial or economic arrangements.

The significant difference from previous social movements is that these will often exploit the infrastructure of informational capitalism—the Internet, the urban habitat, telecommunications, travel—or emerge in new spatial arrangements in urban areas or new nations. (As we have already noted, some religious groups have already made headway on this.) Castells writes:

> Because our historical vision has become so used to historical battalions, colourful banners and scripted proclamations of social change, we are at a loss when confronted with the subtle persuasiveness of incremental changes of symbols processed through multiform networks, away from halls of power.

> It is in these back alleys of society, whether in alternative electronic networks or in grassroots networks of communal resistance, that I have sensed the embryos of a new society, laboured in the fields of history by a new identity. (Castells 1997, 362)

The view is not totally optimistic. One of Castells's concerns is the globalization of crime, which can threaten the economic stability of nations as well as infiltrate the poorest communities through the economies of violence, of drugs and arms, using the same infrastructure as the social movements just mentioned.

The third volume looks to the future. Alongside the need to find ways of checking global crime, Castells identifies three touchstones—the black holes of informational capitalism—on which the global networked society will stand judged. Those touchstones are the plight of Africa—the social and technological exclusion of a whole continent; the communities of the poor in the global North—the continuing exclusion rather than transformation of the urban ghetto in North America and Europe; and the exploitation of children—the exclusion of a generation through exploitation. In a telling sentence concerning the implications of the "dehumanisation of Africa" he writes, "The complex interplay between economy, technology, society and politics [is] the making of a process that denies humanity to African people, as well as to all of us in our inner selves" (Castells 2000b, 83).

Presence and Witness in the Back Alleys

Castells is far from easy or comfortable reading. He poses a challenge to all who are concerned about the future of urban life and community, local and globally, particularly the churches.

That the church is rarely visible in Castells's writings must be a cause for concern. When it does emerge it represents a largely spent or contradictory force, from a fading cultural hegemony—the pope's traditionalist social teaching and its impact on the global South (Castells 2000a, 24) or new fundamentalist movements apparent through their alliances with the world of communication technology (Castells 2000b, 382). This is probably not a failure by Castells to realize the application of his own theses but merely signifies the failure of church and faith groups to realize their potential or develop a new flexibility in the global levels with which he is dealing. One might be justified in asking, however, what of the advance of Christianity in sub-Saharan

Africa, which must surely be critical to the future of the continent? Or the globalization of Pentecostalism, not all of which is allied with the fundamentalist right? (See Cox 1996, or, Dempster, Klaus, and Petersen 1999.)

The political influence of European Christianity may be on the wane; some of its forms may not have yet attained the flexibility vital in a networked global society. But might the shoots of its resurgence visible in new forms be comparable to the social movements of which Castells makes so much? It must surely be in this last group that those concerned with offering an alternative Christian perspective must locate themselves. How, then, do we build up and sustain Christian presence and witness in the back alleys of society or the black holes of informational capitalism?

As we move between local and global neighborhoods we find ourselves interacting with new movements, new ways of thinking and understanding the human condition. These are not just the intellectual developments, which we must engage with the same seriousness with which we are disposed to engage with the new patterns of political, social, and philosophical thought, but social movements. These can include global campaigns such as Greenpeace or Jubilee 2000; campaigns of more localized resistance—the Zapatistas or issue-specific groups, such as those campaigning against the death penalty; causes as diverse as extreme fundamentalism, minority ethnic groups, anticapitalism protests, and fair-trade campaigns. The struggles in the information age are for people's minds, as rigid apparatuses give way to minds mobilized around the power of "flexible, alternative networks":

> This is why identities are so important, and ultimately so powerful in this ever-changing power structure—because they build interests, values and projects around experience, and refuse to dissolve by establishing a specific connection between nature, history, geography and culture. Identities anchor power in some areas of social structure, and build from there their resistance or their offensives in the informational struggle about cultural codes constructing behaviour and, thus, new institutions. (Castells 1997, 360)

These movements, as Castells detects, will often exploit the infrastructure of the urban and global networks using Internet, telecommunications, and technology in a spectrum of causes or acts of resistance, in struggles to overcome the contradictions of identity in the city or to find space for new forms of politics. This phenomenon in some ways repudiates the assumptions that have been considered so far, that globalized change is inevitably driven by corporate economic interests and unstoppable in its current form. The potential of such movements makes globalized urban living so exciting and yet so threatening.

I want to suggest that a church that fails to realize its po-   *
tential in this new context will find itself more and more reduced to individualistic pietism and dogmatic introspection. The strengths of the church must lie in its ability to hold the local and the global in its own dynamic tension, as it seeks the practice of human freedom in the presence of God in whatever human arrangements it encounters at local, national, regional, and global levels. The church needs to understand and realize its potential as it connects and affirms the communities and individuals in the margins of the global city, communities that comprise significant numbers of women, minorities, and migrants—those who really do live on the fault lines and in the back alleys of the new global order. While challenging the reshaping of the geography of power, the Christian faith is lived through presence(s), through communities that include, strengthen, and give integrity to those at the margins. Local pastoral praxis becomes simultaneously global political praxis.

Geographical Literacy and Resistance

We must not fall captive to the simplistic analysis that rejects the global solely for the local—our world is just not like that, and neither is our faith. We need an approach that is willing to take some fairly sophisticated risks, as the stakes are high. To do this, we need to work on our analysis, not least our geographical knowledge.

In March 2000 I was at a lecture given by the geographer David Harvey on the necessity and uses of geographical knowledge: an increasingly urgent acquisition in a world of competing interpretations of globalization and cosmopolitanism. He spoke of how nations, institutions, corporations, and pressure groups produce their own geography—interpreting the world and their place and identity within it. "The social transmission of [geographical knowledge] is vital to the perpetuation or transformation of any social order. It is a vital aspect of power and an object of political and social struggle" (Harvey 2000, 552). Bad, banal, or corrupt geography affects the way the world is understood and the ability to comprehend the intentions of governments and other forces. One of the asides he made (not in the printed version of the lecture) was that during the Central American crisis of the 1980s the only people in the United States who really worked on their geographical literacy were the Central Intelligence Agency (CIA), who were behind much of the destabilizing of the region (demonizing spaces and places for political reasons), and the radical church, who were involved in solidarity and sanctuary work—offering an alternative geography of national interest and security. "New geographies get constructed through political projects, and the production of space is as much a political and moral as a physical fact. The way life gets lived in spaces, places and environments is . . . the beginning and end of political action" (Harvey 2000, 560).

As Christians, we need to be asking ourselves what types of literacy we need at the beginning of the twenty-first century that will help us understand the changes and movements in our world, to read the signs of the time and offer the appropriate challenges.

We will find that many of our challenges remain unanswered with the same frustrations that were visible on the streets of Seattle, Prague, and Davos. Those demonstrations are an important illustration of the potential and the failure of engaging with the global changes that are taking place. But globalization is not a juggernaut to be stopped at all costs; it is a process that can, and must, be subverted through its "lower circuits" as well as adapted, resisted, and guided through whatever access can be found to the higher circuits (see Gunnell and Timms 2000). The potential for faith communities lies in their ability to be present at all levels of global society. But it is particularly in those lower circuits that faith communities can forge new coalitions with other, nonformalized political actors. This will involve those communities developing new, informed geographical understandings of their place and identity.

The recent Jubilee 2000 movement on Third-World debt (whatever its success or failure) has meant that many ordinary Christians have developed a new literacy about the way the world works. And the fusion of Christian ethics and economics must surely take us into new territory when we approach globalization (see Atherton 2000). On a technological level, we might assume that advances in communications and the compression of time and space are inevitable. But on issues relating to economic developments, we must find a way to pose the question: Who does this kind of globalization benefit? We cannot be content to let the inequalities that exist on a micro level in our global cities be tolerated on a macro level throughout the world.

Walter Magnusson has suggested that "the global city is never finished, because new possibilities are always being discovered" (2000, 298). The church's role in the global city may be to identify and nurture new possibilities within the fault lines, back alleys, and lower circuits. In the next chapter we will see how, from the discipline of planning, Leonie Sandercock has written of the need to reshape the education of planners and the praxis of planning. Urban space must be negotiated through layers of economics, culture, religion, and identity. This must also then inform what it means for the church to be present within and alongside the marginal communities that are emerging in this new world situation. In the new city the planner's work must be informed by a new literacy based on the willingness to learn, listen, and dialogue with these communities whose lives are being shaped by many forces, flows, and interests. In the end, however, it will be those subjects who must reimagine the cities of the future (Sandercock 1998).

Notes

1. See, for example, the film *Bread & Roses,* directed by Ken Loach, which documents the undervalorization of the Hispanic cleaners servicing office blocks in downtown Los Angeles.

2. Jubilee 2000's global work is carried on by Jubilee Movement International. See: www.jubilee2000uk.org/jmi/main.htm.

Chapter Four

Shaping Communities for the Urban Future

The Habitat Agenda: A Global Call for Sustainable Communities

The United Nations' Commission on Human Settlements, also known as Habitat, is the key international body concerned with our planet's urban future. The 1996 Habitat II Conference in Istanbul posed important questions about urban settlements and their development. The introduction to the preparatory report *An Urbanizing World* (United Nations 1996) by then-UN Assistant Secretary General Wally N'Dow warns of complacency apparent in governments' approaches to the urban agenda:

> One of the greatest ironies here is that the signs of urbanization are now so evident, so much part of our daily lives, that we have come to take them for granted as part of the "normal" urban scene: the slums and ghettos, the homeless, the paralysing traffic, the poisoning of our urban air and water, drugs, crime, the alienation of our youth, the resurgence of old diseases, such as tuberculosis, and the spread of new ones such as AIDS. Every city knows the signs; every city must fight them. (United Nations 1996, xxi)

As can be seen from this quote, Habitat raises questions on vital aspects of urban life that affect cities across the globe, North and South. The conference posed critical questions about the management of communities. What makes a good urban settlement? How might good governance combine with the concerns of the sustainability program Local Agenda 21 initiated by the Rio Earth Summit (1992)? The Habitat Agenda that came out of the Istanbul conference provides a framework for action and commitments that

promotes "a positive vision of sustainable human settlements—where all have adequate shelter, a healthy and safe
environment, basic services, and productive freely chosen
employment" (Habitat 1996, 19, para. 21). Specific commitments within the agenda include

- Providing access to affordable shelter.
- Making towns, cities, and villages more sustainable—
  socially, economically, and environmentally.
- Enabling broad-based participation in decision making
  and action, including access to justice and community-
  based planning.
- Finding new ways of funding socially inclusive development to counter the problems caused by urbanization.
- The development of "capacity building" programs for
  "civil-society" organizations and groups.
- Improving access to information technology to improve
  awareness of social, economic, and environmental issues and enable national and international exchange on
  practice relevant to the Habitat Agenda. (Habitat 1996)

An important feature of the Habitat program is the recognition that a sustainable urban future cannot be delivered
solely by national or local government but is in the hands of
formal and informal community-based organizations, neighborhood associations, and nongovernment organizations, as
well as individuals. Nicholas You, a UN Habitat coordinator,
has said, "There is a notion that in the long term we all share
the consequences of our individual choices. If a world is a
system of which we are all part then my unsustainable
choices affect the present and the future of everyone" (*CITY*
1996, 83).

Subsequent programs are developing thinking concerning
sustainability and development around three vital issues of
urban governance, secure tenure, and slums. The last of
these is developed with the World Bank as the "Cities Without Slums" program. The Istanbul +5 UN Special Assembly

in June 2001 considered the broader implementation and progress of the Habitat Agenda (UNHCS 2001).

Anyone writing about community, whether it is a city, an organization, a religious community, a church, or a society, needs to identify their appropriateness and sustainability in relation to their historic setting, their relationships with other similar bodies, their relationships with others within their system and in relation to the resources available at present and in the future. An early proponent of sustainability wrote, "The sustainable society offers a new alternative, given three basic provisions: (1) the availability of basic material necessities for all; (2) a far more equitable distribution both internationally and domestically; and (3) a political process characterized by openness and not by repression" (Stivers 1976, 168).

There is much work being done at present in the field of urban planning concerned with the sustainability and the holistic development of urban areas, with an emphasis on beginning with the local and looking for long-term changes through which an area and the community group within it will undergo fundamental and lasting change. Steve Skinner suggests the following questions as a useful way of discerning sustainability within local urban regeneration initiatives:

- Have individual community projects achieved lasting benefits?
- Has the overall initiative tackled the underlying cause of the problem?
- Has there been a wider impact on the long-term behavior of other service providers in the area?
- Are there local structures in place that continue to thrive and contribute to the regeneration of the area after the completion of the life span of the . . . agency?
(Skinner 1997, 10)

A sustainability strategy demands that the total impact of current practices is calculated: economic, environmental, and social. The impact goes well beyond the local community and the immediate area as resources are bought in from global markets, workers travel in from a wide area, waste is dumped with long-term consequences, and the development of communities is affected by the resources available to them. Connecting the economic, the environmental, and the social means that at times sustainability might be technically feasible but will meet with political and economic opposition because of short-term attitudes or vested interests, local or global.

Sustainability thinking suggests ways in which communities need to review the impact they make through their internal life and participation in wider networks. Sustainability integrates concern with ecological resources with questions about wholeness and inclusion, participation and responsibility, social access and the quality of life. Concern with the future gives it an eschatological dimension as resilient communities are developed with a belief that future patterns of life can be different if change is initiated now.

Urban Future 21: Shaping Up for a Competitive Future

An informative, though independent, program in the preparation for the 2001 Habitat +5 Summit was the Urban Future 21 World Commission, which published a report in July 2000. A collaborative project among the governments of Germany, Singapore, Brazil, and South Africa, *Urban 21* offers analysis, prediction, and the prospect of an alternative future addressing many of the concerns raised by the Habitat process (Hall and Pfeiffer 2000). The commissioners divide cities into three types: the city coping with informal hyper growth; the city coping with dynamism; and the weakening mature city, coping with aging.

Much of the report is concerned with offering two scenarios—the current "trend" or "business as usual" scenario, and a "bending the trend" scenario. Without significant intervention by governments and other interests, the sustainability of cities across the world is threatened by overwhelming poverty, environmental problems, or economic stagnation. These trends can be deflected if governments act positively but sensitively to influence the driving forces. Education, environmental controls, transport, governance, flexibility in housing, pensions, and taxation are seen as key in the strategies to be developed. Negotiation is vital if cities are to be livable—between the haves and have-nots, between different ethnic groups, between the technologists and the technically illiterate. Influxes of new inhabitants, particularly from places without any urban tradition, are seen as making the development of any civil infrastructure perplexing. There is a pervading sense of urgency: "Sociologists have come to recognize that sociable urban living requires generations of inculcated habit. Yet waiting all that time is a luxury these cities and their people cannot afford. They have very definite expectations of what they want from urban life, though these may not always be realistic" (Hall and Pfeiffer 2000, 16).

The outlook is basically optimistic. Development of skills and entry into the formal economy are expected to bring millions of people out of poverty into relative affluence. There is an underlying hope that technological advance and globalization will prove benign forces in global development and that enlightened self-interest will win the day. This approach feeds the assumption that, through competition, cities develop and succeed, moving upward through the three classifications. The inevitability of winners and losers in the process, and the prospects for those on the losing-end terms of cities, and individuals in cities, are not fully articulated.

There is much in *Urban 21* that cannot be ignored; the wealth of detail is staggering, and the analysis is vital. The report has welcome insights into issues of environmental sustainability and transport as well as the need to connect these with issues of disease prevention and primary health care. But there is a need for others to develop analysis and research that bring players like the Urban 21 Commission into dialogue. The fate of our cities is too important to leave to the few government-funded initiatives and far too important to leave to a *laissez-faire* global market. The interests behind certain aspects of urbanization and globalization need to be critiqued and exposed—are there significant powers who are interested in keeping things the way they are?

Urban 21 seems primarily concerned with urban infrastructure into which populations will fit; while it explores how the urban population might be engaged in the planning of its built environment and that infrastructure, such an approach seems to be new territory. Obviously in some places clean water, access to public transport, and secure tenure remain priorities that are best addressed through community-government partnerships, but this still fails to address the spatial division of the city and the questions of social access and capability. The forms of city governance will often reflect the assumptions of top-down management rather than the potential of new alliances that include the poor as part of the solution and are not reluctant to use social justice as their driving force. Radical urbanologist Peter Marcuse connects this dilemma with the concerns of our next commentator:

> hierarchy is not an inevitable part of social organisation. We live in a society in which the prosperity of one is often based on the poverty of the other. That need not be so, we have today the resources, the skills, the room, to be able to combine justice with prosperity, mutual respect with efficient organization. Physical rearrangements, restructuring can help achieve such a society; attacking walls of domination, walls of confinement, will help. But they need to be part of a broader effort to build a better society, physically, economically, socially, politically. (Marcuse 1994, 251)

Leonie Sandercock: Planning and Justice in Cosmopolis

The planning of our urban areas must be a discipline in which those concerned with the shape of the cities of the future can engage. The monolith cities of planning theory have little in common with the urban populations that are emerging shaped by migration and new minorities with their multiple layers of expectation and energy. The demands for new types of space on a human scale must force a reassessment of how planning and architecture are discussed and exercised. Pluralism poses the greatest challenge to the practice of planning, with its enlightenment and modernist assumptions, which has led to socially and ethnically polarized cities where planning is primarily capital-led, often concerned with grandiose commercial or high-culture projects. Australian planner Leonie Sandercock not only criticizes the false division of planning and architecture in the schools of North America and the UK and the assumption that either can be practiced from a politically neutral standpoint but also declares the need for a foundational critical theory informed by postmodernism, feminism, and postcolonialism. "Planning has never been value-neutral. It ought now to be explicitly value-sensitive, working on behalf of the most vulnerable groups in multicultural cities and regions, accommodating rather than eradicating difference" (Sandercock 1998b, 206). A new awareness is needed of the changes and opportunities that exisit in urban communities—the rise of civil society, and new communities being formed through transnational migration and the emergence of new community identities in "cities of difference."

Sandercock traces the recent history of planning practice and its epistemological base. She dissects its attempts to impose and define the spirit of urban communities from the top down, with its appeals to ill-defined notions of public interest and civic welfare. Globalization is a local, community phenomenon; the world city is defined not only by its financial and technological connections but also through the diversity of its inhabitants. Urban space must be negotiated through layers of economics, culture, religion, and identity. In the new city the planner's work must be informed by a new literacy based on the willingness to learn, listen, and dialogue with the communities whose lives are being molded. In the end, however, it will be those subjects who must shape the cities of the future. Cities cannot go on the way they are. Sandercock's vision is glimpsed in "a thousand tiny empowerments" in the cross-community action of Boston's Rainbow Coalition; the Popular Education Center in Los Angeles; the struggles of the Wik people of the Cape York Peninsula, Australia; Frankfurt's Municipal Department of Multicultural Affairs; and the People's Budget Process of Porto Alegre. These programs offer direct access to capacity building and decision making for those most affected by the changes initiated in their communities. The human dimension of the global city is where people can learn to live with each other, concerned with the quality of life and its sustainability, where negotiation plays a full part in the process of transformation. Those negotiations must recognize the difference in and draw on the richness of those layers if the city is to have a future, if it is to move toward *Cosmopolis*. The management of urban society does not have to be based on containment, control, and manipulation (Sandercock 2000).

✳   *Cosmopolis* is the city where people live with, make room for, and celebrate difference; it is "a postmodern Utopia . . . a construction site of the mind, a city/region in which there is genuine connection with, and respect and space for the cultural Other, and the possibility of working together on matters of common destiny, a recognition of intertwined fates" (Sandercock 1998b, 164). Her vision of *Cosmopolis* offers possibility to the planner, demanding a paradigmatic shift away from the assumptions of the modernist city toward alternative epistemologies found in communities of diversity, struggle, and hope. "Local communities have grounded experiential, intuitive contextual knowledges which are often more manifested in stories, songs, visual images and speech than in typical planning sources. Insurgent planners need to learn and practise these in other ways" (Sandercock 1998b, 205). For planning to be ethical "the public interest" must be deconstructed and replaced by Sandercock's new paradigm of "negotiating fears and anxieties, mediating memories and hopes, and facilitating change and transformation" (Sandercock 2000, 44), a praxis based on discretion and imagination. Sandercock is intensely concerned with the praxis of the planner, reawakening a sense of action synonymous with change. It is a matter of profession and vocation through which a new way of creating robust and sustainable urban communities must emerge. Solidarity is critical; from solidarity the critique will emerge. "The most promising experiments in insurgent planning have involved mobilized communities forging coalitions to work for broad objectives of economic, environmental, social and cultural justice, and in the process resisting, engaging with and participating in the state" (Sandercock 1998b, 218).

Sandercock's vision is passionate and full of conviction about how cities are and what they might become. As well as reimagining planning it demands "new concepts of social justice, citizenship, community and shared interest" (Sandercock 1998b, 125). Yet Sandercock's is also an audacious challenge to all those whose professions are bound up with shaping the world's urban future—planners, architects, community workers, and faith leaders. Are the services, the solidarity, and the critiques they offer really concerned with the possibility of community and hope in such new and dynamic incarnations? Sandercock's challenge concludes with the following *cri de coeur:*

> I dream of a city where action is synonymous with change; where social justice is . . . prized . . . where I have a right to my surroundings and so do all my fellow citizens; where no one flaunts authority and no one is without authority; where I don't have to translate my "expertise" to impress officials and confuse citizens. . . .
>
> I want a city where my profession contributes to all of [this] . . . where city planning is a war of liberation fought against dumb, featureless public space as well as the multiple sources of oppression and domination and exploitation and violence; where citizens wrest from space new possibilities, and immerse themselves in their cultures while respecting those of their neighbours, and

collectively forging new hybrid cultures and spaces. (Sandercock
1998b, 219)

Renegotiating the City

✳ Sandercock touches on the need to "resacralize" the spatiality and ecology of the city as part of insurgent planning
strategies, which defy the imposition of "dumb, featureless
public space . . . devoid of the spirit" (Sandercock 1998b,
212–14, 219; also 1998a). Like Jane M. Jacobs, she points to
the secular assumptions of postmodern urban theory and
how this merely perpetuates Western, modernist assumptions and the cultures of colonial urbanism (Jacobs 1996,
131). The spirit of a place is engendered as much by the community of the present as the stories of the past that are
brought there. Too often planners have been solely concerned with issues of infrastructure in design assuming
"community" will follow and not with engaging the community that will fill that space—and this is even more vital with
the "multistoried" communities that now exist in cities. A
metaphorical removal of shoes must surely be a prerequisite
for those who approach the places in which others have
found meaning and "lodged" their stories. The use of cultural activities within the regeneration process is often advocated as a way of enabling histories to be shared and enabling
new histories to be created in new communities. These
exercises can be essential in early stages of reimagining a
community's built environment allowing a greater sense of
confidence and stake holding in the planning process to
develop (see Landry 1996).

The lessons of modernist planning, which supposedly created so many terrains that were "devoid of the spirit," are
that urban populations will adapt or reshape (sometimes de-
structively) a built environment into which they have been
coerced and which militates against diverse human flourish-
ing. Authentic urban space is contested, but that contestation can be negotiated and creative if it takes place in the
human arena; it should not be a battle between people and

an imposed built environment. This is not simply a question of rights but also of conviction, as to why and for what the urban community exists. A recent collaborative commentary on British urban policy makes this point:

> we have stressed the rights of being, becoming and interconnecting in the city; rights that do not flow alone from the ways in which the physical space is organised, but also from the development and expressive opportunities given to people. But as such, our interest has been less in the search for a common good or consensus—an impossible challenge in the heterogeneous city—than in ways in which living together in cities is an enriching creative experience. (Amin, Massey, and Thrift 2000, 45)

Living Cosmopolis

The new paradigm for planning that Sandercock advocates is mediated and sustained in what liberation theologians have taught us in praxis where theory, reflection, and action combine, subject to the critique of marginal communities for whom change is a matter of life or death (Gutiérrez 1980, 22). Praxis demands an ideological underpinning, matched by personal commitment. For example, put the words of the Argentine philosopher-theologian Enrique Dussel alongside the vision that emerges from Sandercock's vision: "Praxis is the actualization of proximity, of the experience of being proximate, for one's neighbor. Praxis is the experience of constructing the other as person, as the end of my action and not as means. We are dealing with a relationship of infinite respect" (Dussel 1988, 9).

As a theologian I find common ground in Sandercock's vision of *Cosmopolis*. The theological notions of *koinonia* (solidarity/mutuality) and, to use what remains a problematic patriarchal phrase, the kingdom are concerned with the practice of new, defiant patterns of social relationships that draw on the ideal—already but not yet: that is "on earth, as it is in heaven" (see chap. 6). As with *Cosmopolis* we are dealing with a utopian critique that "can never be realized, but must always be in the making" (Sandercock 1998b, 163) but should be glimpsed in the life and struggles of those who make claim to it. *Cosmopolis* is a critique that may be articulated or actualized in the praxis of communities and movements who refuse to let existing arrangements persist or the interests of the few shape the future; it is a resistance that must ultimately take spatial, material forms shaped, guided, and built by their communities.

These notions demand an inclusivity in the processes that shape the communities that are initiated, an affirmation of those excluded by other communities, and a radical reordering of resources. The kingdom, in the teaching and praxis of Jesus, is about the creation of space for such possibilities to be imagined.

Addressing the layers of difference and distance that we encounter in global urban society must challenge the way our theology negotiates and speaks alongside and within the diverse, competing, conflicting cultural claims on the future. These spaces of urban negotiation are described by Edward Soja as "third space"—an arena like Sandercock's *Cosmopolis* where theory and practice are reimagined—alternatives are trailed, space negotiated, and communities of resistance are formed. Soja gives as an example the work of African American writer bell hooks, who "attempts to move beyond modernist binary oppositions of race, gender and class into the multiplicity of *other* spaces that difference makes; into a re-visioned spatiality that creates from difference new sites for struggle and for the construction of interconnected and non-exclusionary communities of resistance" (Soja 1996, 96).

In defining her cultural politics of difference and identity, hooks exploits and engages the language of marginality. While some would understand the margins as a place of confinement and repression, such as is apparent in the segregation of urban space on an ethnic and socioeconomic basis, the margins for her become a site of encounter and resistance—enhanced by the refusal to accept the imposition of others' definitions and categories. "For hooks, the political project is to occupy the (real-and-imagined) spaces on the margins" to reclaim and call others into the "radically open and openly radical" place from which change becomes possible (Soja 1996, 99–100). "Marginality is the space of resistance. Enter that space. Let us meet there. Enter that space. We greet you as liberators" (hooks 1990, 152, quoted by Soja 1996, 152).

In the next section I want to explore how marginality often provokes the scriptural paradigms of engagement with urban experience and how those paradigms might inform the church's praxis in the twenty-first-century city.

Part Two

Urban Experience and Biblical Space

Chapter Five

Reimaging the Biblical City

Urban Places and Movements in Biblical Space

In what ways might the Bible be used to help us understand the urban experience better? We should not expect a blueprint for urban living; yet if we are prepared to make a leap of imagination into the world that shaped the writers of Scripture, we encounter many familiar attitudes and reactions to the urban context and its impact on a wider society. The preindustrial cities of the ancient Near Eastern world were, obviously, very different from our own, yet at the same time the impact and lure of urbanism shaped the inhabitants of the region and their faith in a number of fundamental ways. Urbanization is a biblical reality. The experience of God's people recounted in both Testaments is often in the shadow of the rapid social change associated with the role of human settlements. The encounter with the urban is also a global encounter involving movement and contestation in the local setting and across a larger arena—the forced journey to another place (exile), resettlement (as the exiles returned), invasion and colonization by a foreign power (the Greek and Roman occupation of the land), or transnational flows (the interaction of the network of early Christian communities).

As residents or strangers, people of faith are called to form countercommunities existing in the shadow of power. We see how captive, prophetic, exilic, remnant, messianic, and apocalyptic communities develop according to adaptable understandings of that power and the cities in which they live and witness. In the Psalms there is a mandate to pray for the peace of the provincial cultic city of Jerusalem, yet the experience of resisting the massive urban settlements of Egypt and Babylon formed the Hebrew story and religion in the most significant fashion. In the second Testament the ministry of Jesus emerges from the shadows of the colonial urbanism of the Roman Empire; later it is in the world cities of Athens, Alexandria, and Rome where the growing church discovers its missionary base as well as its antipathy to the dominant urban culture (places where to seek the city's civil good would lead to compromise in the midst of a pagan culture).

There is no great "urban narrative" in the Bible that takes us from the city of Cain (Gen 4) to the New Jerusalem (Rev 21), in much the same way that urban histories of the twentieth century take us from Athens to Chicago or Los Angeles. However, urbanism is present throughout Scripture as an influence, casting a shadow, pulling, challenging, devouring, provoking a response. The protagonists and writers wrestle with those forces, processes, and movements in rural and wilderness settings as well as within the multiple layers of urban life.

In what ways can the urban experience be discerned in the processes that shape the faith and theology we find in the Bible? To answer that, we need to understand a little of the social setting in which the traditions were conceived, handed down, and finally edited. For the most part, the writing we have will have an urban spin as it was within the urban literate community that the final editorial work on the texts took place. To discern what was really happening will mean reading between the lines and supplementing what we find with the work of archaeologists and social historians. If we are determined to look for the experience of the poor through the urban experience of Scripture we may find ourselves delving into the realms of antihistory, engaging suspicion as a vital interpretative tool as we ask the question: Were things really as they are portrayed? Cities are the locale of ruling élites, of kings and their functionaries, with their constant demands for economic and agricultural resources. At times the urban order might be understood only in terms of such negative impact, much in the way that many groups consider globalization at the beginning of the twenty-first century. Look, for example, at the arguments offered by the prophet Samuel against a centralized urban monarchy (1 Sam 8).

The Hebrew Bible

Despite the statements about the first cities that we find in the early part of Genesis, the chapters that concern origins and prehistory can offer us no insights into the origin of urban life. Through the excavation of Neolithic sites such as Çatal Hoyuk, in Anatolia, urban archaeology has thrown up a number of questions concerning settlement, agriculture, and trade six thousand years before the setting of the ancestral narratives of Abraham and Sarah.[1] The cities we do encounter in those narratives are centered on a few settled societies in the Levant and the single megapower of Egypt, in an era toward the end of the first urban revolution. In the ancestral narratives, urbanism is associated with a form of settled power and society that has been rejected and in which the ancestors do not have a place. They stand on the edge and yet are integral to the welfare of urban communities: unsettling the court of Pharaoh (Gen 12), interceding for the settlements of the plain (Gen 18), intervening to save the Egyptian cities from famine (Gen 41).

Elsewhere the Hebrew Scriptures often leave us with stark, apocalyptic images of the city being shaken, under judgment. From his urban exile Ezekiel described "the bloody city" as a place of idols and the abuse of human dignity:

> You, mortal, will you judge, will you judge the bloody city? Then declare to it all its abominable deeds. Its officials within it are like wolves tearing the prey, shedding blood, destroying lives to get dishonest gain. . . . The people of the land have practiced extortion and committed robbery; they have oppressed the poor and needy, and have extorted from the alien without redress. (Ezek 22:2, 27–29)

The prophet saw the city as the place where order breaks down, where survival takes precedence over morality, and where identity and traditions are lost and expectations clash; as a consuming organism devouring not just its own inhabitants but all those who are vulnerable, those within its sphere of influence. Elsewhere cities take on personas—usually female, "lasciviously promiscuous or adulterous," whose behavior is to be condemned (Isa 23:15–17; Day 1995). For instance, Jeremiah refers to Jerusalem as bride (Jer 2:2), whore (Jer 2:20), and faithless wife (Jer 3:20).

* Yet throughout the prophets we find the conviction that the urban, however corrupted, can be restored, regenerated, and redeemed, that it can be home to the exile, that it can offer sanctuary to the stranger and justice to the oppressed and persecuted. Walter Brueggemann, when reflecting on land theologies, wrote, "a sense of place is a primary category of faith" (Brueggemann 1977, 4). Space becomes place only when there are stories and hopes lodged there. The experience of exile and captivity is the experience of coerced space in contrast with trusted place. "The central problem is not emancipation but rootage, not meaning but belonging, not separation from community but location within it" (Brueggemann 1977, 187).

The cities of the kingdoms of Israel and Judah rarely warrant that designation through their size or economic impact. Ancient forms of Hebrew never developed or adopted a special word for "city" in the Greek sense but used 'ir for cities, towns, and villages alike (Smith 1987, 50; VanGemeren 1997, 396–99), so there is a need to examine archaeological and textual data before using the urban assumption for the settlements that are mentioned. Jerusalem dominates these settlements, culturally and politically, as it becomes the center of a basic tributary system of government. Its significance as a military and administrative center predates the conquest by David; its absorption into the emergent kingdom provided the administrative base he was desperately in need of. Jorge Pixley considers as highly significant the fact that the inhabitants of Jerusalem were not put to the sword, as had been the case with other Canaanite cities. The population of Jerusalem provided "a quarry of government officials for the new King of Israel" (Pixley 1992, 33).[2] The ensuing tensions that arose between the ruling urban élites of Jerusalem and Samaria, and the agricultural populace, are easily discernible in the historical and prophetic writings (e.g., Mic 1:5). As those tensions increased, the only solution to some radicals became the destruction of the cities and the system that sustained them (Amos 2:5; Hos 13:16).

> Hear this, you rulers of the house of Jacob and chiefs of the house of Israel, who abhor justice and pervert all equity, who build Zion with blood and Jerusalem with wrong! Its rulers give judgment for a bribe, its priests teach for a price, its prophets give oracles for money; yet they lean upon the LORD and say, "Surely the LORD is with us! No harm shall come upon us." Therefore because of you Zion shall be plowed as a field; Jerusalem shall become a heap of ruins, and the mountain of the house a wooded height. (Mic 3:9–12)

Babylon and Nineveh are cities of the imagination, of a size and an order of which exiles and prophets had no previous experience or comprehension. It was an encounter with a unique form of urbanism; despotic and cultic ideologies apparent as much in the spatial layout of the city as in its social stratification (see Van De Mieroop 1997). The staggering description of Nineveh as being "three days' walk across" (Jonah 3:3) bears no relation to the archaeological evidence, yet it communicates the narrator's awe at an urban form he has no way of categorizing.[3] Jeremiah and Jonah both develop a theology of vocation to communities in which the people of God are not part of the ruling hegemony but are called to actively pursue the welfare and salvation of places in which they have no claim. In Jonah's case the problem turns out to be the prophet, not the city. Whether "standing on the edge" like Jonah or Abraham, or living as a minority, the community of faith must seek its welfare through enhancing that of others.

> But seek the welfare of the city where I have sent you into exile, and pray to the LORD on its behalf, for in its welfare you will find your welfare. (Jer 29:7)

> What a way to welfare, that hated Babylon is the place of well-being. Thus exile is not only the place of unexpected word. It is also the place of unexpected unacceptable vocation—exiles seeking welfare for others! Seek only justice and righteousness, even in anxiety, and get the kingdom (Matt 6:33). Seek *shalom,* and you'll get the land. (Brueggemann 1977, 126)

But Babylon could not be home. The Jeremiah who advocated coexistence is later heard to dismiss the city as beyond redemption, beyond healing (Jer 51:8–9).

Despite the experience of exile, a familiar pattern emerges as Jerusalem is rebuilt under Persian rule. Nehemiah returns to Jerusalem with an agenda that goes well beyond the restoration of the city's walls and built environment (Neh 1–4). Jerusalem is contested as the returnees from Babylon vie for space and control with the residual population. Populist measures on issues of economic exploitation and monetary justice are dealt with succinctly (Neh 5), giving Nehemiah a political security that would later drive forward an ethnic purity program (Neh 9:2; 10:28) and spatial intimidation and coercion (Neh 11:25–36), as Jerusalem was gentrified to meet the expectations of the returned élite (Neh 11:1–24). Later, this is reinforced as the rebuilding of the temple introduces a new element of coercion as cultic participation is linked to property rights (Ezek 11:15).

The postexilic, city-based administration emerges with the reestablished temple as its *raison d'être,* and the codification of that domination is embarked upon as the traditions of the people are edited into a single *torah* by the returned urban élite. The conflict between this élite and others, many of whom had stayed in Jerusalem during the exile, came to its literary climax in the struggle over the prophetic tradition. As the Levitical order tightened its control of the temple, claiming specificity and allegiance for its location, studious dissidents began adding codicils, often anonymously, to prophetic writings that looked forward to the regeneration of Jerusalem and a new outpouring of the Spirit (Pixley 1992, 120–23).

Arise, shine; for your light has come, and the glory of the LORD has risen upon you. For darkness shall cover the earth, and thick darkness the peoples; but the LORD will arise upon you, and his glory will appear over you. Nations shall come to your light, and kings to the brightness of your dawn. (Isa 60:1–3)

In subsequent years the urban space of Palestine was to be contested and reshaped by new social forces and cultural intruders. Hellenization eclipsed the cultural supremacy of Egypt and Persia. This was primarily a gradual cultural infiltration well before the military conquest by Alexander in 332 B.C.E. and subsequent attempts at colonization. The Hellenizers introduced Greek notions of the city with its civic and cultic life, different forms of property tenure, and legal compliance (see Smith 1987). Small colony cities with distinct orders of patronage introduced an incipient form of urbanization. New patterns of resistance—literary, spatial, and violent—were developed by a subject people, even though they were often ideologically and theologically fragmented. The experience was to remold Judaism. Ellis Rivkin comments:

> The ongoing process of urbanization had so altered the structure of the experience of merchant, shopkeeper, artisan, and peasant alike that the Pentateuch no longer resonated with their deepest needs and their innermost yearnings. For the Pentateuch had been designed for a relatively simple agricultural–priestly society and not a complex urban–agricultural society embedded within a world of *poleis*. . . . When therefore a crisis of leadership occurred . . . the people were ripe not merely for rebellion but revolution. (quoted in Lee 1995, 22)

These forces culminated first in the revolt led by the Maccabees and later in the sectarian and spatial fragmentation of Judaism.

Notes

1. See Çatal Hoyuk Research Project web page: http://catal.arch .cam.ac.uk/catal/catal.html. For explorations of the implications of Çatal Hoyuk for urban studies see Jacobs 1970 and Soja 2000.

2. However, Keith Whitlam warns "that there is no Hebrew term which corresponds to the city of David as 'capital,' " and attempts to read back such constructions into the biblical narrative are dangerous, when the constitution of ancient Israel is so disputed. Whitelam asserts that the "intertextual construction of Jerusalem as the Davidic capital of monarchic Israel reflecting the image of modern European states and their capitals" relates closely "to the competing claims to Jerusalem as contemporary capital." The construction of Jerusalem in narrative and image illustrates the contention that space is "a product literally filled with ideologies." See "Constructing Jerusalem" available on the website of the SBL/AAR Constructions of Ancient Space Seminar at: www .gunnzone.org/constructs/whitelam.htm#44. A shorter version of the article is available in Greenspoon 2002.

3. "The reader is not supposed to do arithmetic. He is supposed to be lost in astonishment": H. W. Wolff, quoted in Limberg 1993, 78.

Chapter Six

Jesus: An Encounter with Urban Galilee and Jerusalem

Urbanization in Galilee—and Its Discontents

A superficial reading of the Gospel narrative might suggest that the Jesus movement has its origins in a rural context in northern Palestine, with little impact in the urban cultic center of Jerusalem until late in the story. The Roman occupation of Palestine is similarly read as "a little local difficulty," a provincial rural backwater where resistance might be offered by a few fanatics. Archaeology suggests a more complex picture that rings true with a closer reading of the text. The Roman provinces of the eastern Mediterranean were on the fringes of the greatest globalization and urbanization projects of the ancient world.

Andrew Wallace-Hadrill has written, "When it comes to imposing order on the barbarians, the Romans left no doubt of their commitment to the town as an instrument of civilisation. Urbanisation is the unmistakable result of Roman control" (Wallace-Hadrill 1992, 249). Palestine was no exception. In Galilee, the peasant settlements of Nazareth, Capernaum, and Bethsaida stood with the fishing hamlets and farms in the shadow of new settlements—Sepphoris, Tiberias, and Magdala, Hellenized Jewish cities developed by the Herodian client rulers, particularly Herod Antipas (ruled 4 B.C.E.–39 C.E.). Not so far away were a number of colonial cities, the Decapolis, with even stronger Greek urban cultures. Marianne Sawicki writes that "Tiberias in the 20s of the first century C.E., was becoming an international commercial hub for the promotion of agribusiness and industrial expansion" (Sawicki 2000, 134). The domination of those cities was a vital factor in the social environment in which Jesus grew up. The tight-knit village community might have provided basic, informal religious, educational, and welfare structures, but the new cities would have been where it was necessary to lodge property claims, settle legal disputes, consult rabbinical authorities, find markets or even work. Coming from a family associated with the construction trade (a *tekton* [Mark 6:3; Matt 13:55] seems best translated "construction craftsman") it seems plausible that much of Jesus' father's career, as well as his own early life, might have been spent laboring on these construction projects close to his home village (Sawicki 1994, 31).[1]

Jesus' speeches and stories are littered with images of construction and the economic demands of the city with its requirements for larger harvests (Luke 12:18), the need to estimate before embarking on a building project (Luke 14:28), the construction of unsafe towers (Luke 13:4) and houses (Matt 7:26), the references to cities built on hills (Matt 5:14), and venality of urban tax collectors. The new towns relied on the peasant economy to meet their needs at the lowest possible price, exacerbating the poverty of the lean year in the agricultural worker's struggle for survival. "The pressure of world markets and imperial taxation was felt everywhere" (Sawicki 1994, 13).

> Roman urbanization . . . dislocated the traditional peasant way of life and pushed individuals from poverty into destitution, from small landowner into tenant farmer, from tenant farmer into day labourer, and from day labourer into beggar or bandit. (Crossan 1998, 223)

> The economic strain that Antipas's building of Sepphoris and Tiberias placed on the rest of Galilee is difficult to determine on an absolute scale, as is the resulting poverty level and sense of security. It is not necessary to envision an extreme crisis in Galilee—peasant life in antiquity was difficult enough and need not be exaggerated. It is, however, important to stress that Antipas's urbanization of Galilee began a process in which the latter state was perceived as worse than the former by the vast majority; in other words, the peasants' relative state of depriva-

tion, not their poverty in any absolute terms, is the decisive factor. (Reed 2000, 97)

In the parable of the sower (Mark 4:3–20) we find a miraculous harvest that will enable the hopeless tenant farmer to liberate himself from the urban, absentee landowner (Myers 1988, 176–77): the first-century peasant equivalent of winning the lottery, with probably the same odds. The builder of larger granaries gives little thought to those from the villages whose labor would fill them. We hear of rulers and landowners that are absent from their estates (Mark 13:34–35) and a class of managers who exploit the situation (Luke 12:42–48). In many aspects, the ministry of Jesus took place on and within these local and global social tensions.

While E. P. Sanders states that one of the facts of Jesus' public career that is almost beyond dispute is that "he taught in the towns, villages and countryside of Galilee (apparently not the cities)" (Sanders 1993, 10), others argue that as the influence of those cities on the setting in which Jesus operated is beyond question, the situation may not be as easily delineated. The synoptic Galilean ministry of Jesus rarely enters the urban environment—Sepphoris is never even mentioned; those urban centers that are mentioned are referred to as regional interests through which Jesus passed, such as the territories of Tyre and Sidon or the Decapolis region, rather than locations of preaching and healing. These were colonial Gentile cities, while Tiberias and Sepphoris were Galilean/Jewish, though more Hellenized, with less Aramaic spoken, and more affluent than the lakeside settlements such as Capernaum and Bethsaida. More significantly, however, Sepphoris and Tiberias were also political centers—carrying associations with the suppression and execution of John the Baptist. Judging by Jesus' dismissal of Antipas as "that fox" (Luke 13:31–33), who was intent on killing him, these cities may have been avoided for primarily political reasons (Reed 2000, 137–38).

As the demands of those cities were drawing on the resources of the Galilean countryside at an unprecedented level, the economy and politics of the area were increasingly orientated toward the spheres of urban influence and their demands. Sean Freyne identifies the wide use of coinage in Galilee among all social groups (evident through archaeology as well as the Gospels) as the most significant social shift of that time (Freyne 1995). The use of coinage assumes access to urban markets and a flow of goods and assets between settlements. Money provided the means to administer tax and tribute systems as well as rents and tithes; however, "its use in the Gospels consistently points to an asymmetrical system of exchange" (Reed 2000, 98).

The Romans, the Herodians, the landlords, and the temple all took their portion of peasant resources, leading not just to a permanent layer of debt but also ritual impurity and anxiety. The inability to fulfill their financial obligations to the temple cult meant many peasants were considered impure—the productivity of the land was thought to be dependent on the purity of those who tilled it, so the peasantry found themselves caught up in a cycle of taboo, guilt, and impoverishment. "The Lord's Prayer crystallizes the essential peasant concern by praying for the release from debt" (Reed 2000, 97). The *torah* should have provided a safeguard, tying the fortunes of the temple to the practice of justice in the land, "an expression of God's covenant, a way of ensuring that God's land would be a haven of justice in an unjust world" (Herzog 2000, 109). Jesus taps into the latent prophetic tradition of the north, through offering a critique of the centrist, rapacious orientation of the religious system; those who should have been concerned with the purity of the land perpetuated a system of injustice. William Herzog makes this illuminating comment on the predators in the parable of the sower:

> They represent the forces that attempt to devour, scorch, and choke the fruitful land. The problem, then, is neither the lack of compliance in fulfilling the purity codes or the refusal to pay tithes. The problem is with the rapacious and greedy who devour the peasants' crops and choke their efforts to make ends meet. To blame their scarcity on their ability to fulfill the Torah

is to distract the peasants from the true source of their poverty, the ruling elites who take almost everything and leave almost nothing. (Herzog 2000, 195)

The message of Jesus addresses all who were caught up in this spiral of debt and injustice: peasants, artisans, retainers, managers; those who bore the brunt of the system and the intermediaries, the key links in extracting all the rural areas could give but who acted as buffers for the hostility inherent in the system.

The Jesus movement offered an alternative to the debt-ridden, urban-centered economy and "the increased visibility between haves and have-nots" (Reed 2000, 136). Through the declaration of "God's new order" (to use a phrase that overcomes problematic "kingdom" or "reign" phraseology) and the reimagining of *torah,* Jesus intervenes in the false order that distorts and divides the people of God and the processes that through devalorization create people who are outcasts and excluded. The offering of forgiveness and the cancellation of debt are the essential activities of God's new order. There can be no conflict between love of God and love of neighbor: to put one above the other is to create a bogus dilemma. By placing material justice through debt cancellation at the heart of his message, Jesus is warning his listeners and followers against imitating and internalizing the culture that has enslaved them.

A Space for Justice

Rehabilitation and restoration are an essential part of many encounters of marginal people with Jesus. The unclean and dispossessed are cleansed and told to "go home," to rejoin the community from which they come as full, whole members— to repossess their inheritance, their home space (Mark 2:11; 5:19). The act of healing thus becomes a threat to those who have exploited another's misfortune and moved into their space. On the other side there are those who must be dispossessed or challenged to become dispossessed of the security in which their position or future is vested (Matt 19:16–28). The resistance Jesus meets is primarily from those who have most to lose if space and material resources are to be so radically reordered (see Brueggemann 1997, 171ff.).

Among such marginal people Jesus stimulates faith; he encourages them to comprehend the reality of what makes them marginal. They are receptive not only to the message but also to the invitation to create an alternative way of community life, on the periphery, which challenges the hegemony that others wittingly and unwittingly maintain; this new community Crossan calls the "kingdom of nobodies and nuisances" (Crossan 1994, 54). This symbolic action (not least at the symbolic level of ritual ideas about impurity) is in essence political action. Christopher Rowland suggests a way of understanding the political nature of Jesus' actions:

> By political in this context I mean their relationship to conventional patterns of human interaction and organisation, whether formal (like a Sanhedrin or local body of elders) or informal and traditional (like widely established practices). The political challenge posed by Jesus involved departures from norms of behaviour, status, attitude and access to social intercourse which are typical of a particular society. (Rowland 1993, 240)

Political action takes such clandestine forms when the majority of the population is excluded from any type of structural political participation.

Herzog reads Jesus' parables of the mustard seed (Mark 4:31–32) and the yeast (Matt 13:33) as defiant statements about the contagious and contaminating nature of God's new order and its ideology, maybe even commandeering the derogatory language of his enemies (Herzog 2000, 25–27). God's new order is about the reclamation of human space as the arena for economic and social justice; about the overvalorization of people, places, and activities contrary to the value placed upon them by the cultic leaders, their urban masters, or their Roman overlords. Walter Brueggemann puts this in terms of utility and valorization:

The radicalness of this ministry is of course in the calling into question those norms and values which serve to enfranchise and disenfranchise. (Brueggemann 1977, 174)

The production-consumption values inevitably place a central priority upon utility, upon reward for people who can perform useful tasks. Such values tend to discard people without utility. And Jesus, the center of land-history, announced and embodied the conviction that in the new land (the kingdom) the issue of utility as a means of entry was not pertinent (cf. Luke 14:12–14, 21–24). (Brueggemann 1977, 194)

Contesting Jerusalem

Jesus' assault comes to a head in Jerusalem, the arena where he confronts the religious and political powers. God's new order "necessitated a radical response to the divine, which eventually led to a critique of most contemporary religious expressions within Judaism, even of the priestly apparatus and the Temple in Jerusalem" (Reed 2000, 220).

The symbolism of Jerusalem is immediately apparent as the city combined the locus of the administrative and the cultic power that God's new order contests. The city's story was antiprophet (Matt 23:37) and represented the challenge and danger faced by those who would be faithful to alternative systems of rule.

Jesus' prophetic action in the outer courts of the temple operates at a number of levels. His own impurity could well have meant that this was the furthest he was able to enter. By attacking the traders he breaks a link in the economic flow of resources into the central treasuries ("the street level representatives of banking interests of considerable power"— maybe the capital that was amassed was then used in further loans adding another layer of indebtedness) (Myers 1988, 300–301; Herzog 2000, 141). The activity and system they were part of contaminated the space around them just as leprosy was supposed to infect the stones of the sufferer's home (Lev 14:33–53); the only course of action could be the destruction of the temple and the reordering of its space according to God's new order.

The subsequent show trial and execution of Jesus, on charges concerning the payment of tribute, cursing the temple, and sedition, followed its inevitable course, contrived by the secular and cultic authorities. The ensuing events and movement took the empowering presence of Jesus and the message of God's new order into an urban environment in which the accounts of a life that incarnated divine justice were retold and inspired new generations of disciples.

Notes

1. According to one ancient source (Origen), Jesus may have even been a migrant building laborer in Egypt (see Rousseau and Arav 1996, 340).

Chapter Seven

Retelling and Living the Story of Jesus in an Urban World

From Galilee to a Cosmopolitan World

The notions we have of the message and life of Jesus come from excavating the data we have in the Gospels, near-contemporary writings, and archaeological evidence. In that process we also encounter the first Christians: behind the Gospel writers and in the letters of Paul we glimpse a church striving to come to terms with its memory of radical relationships away from its Palestinian origins. As new communities they were striving for a common identity. Like many urban congregations of today, early Christian congregations were heterogeneous assortments of peoples attempting to bond and create a sustainable community life, often against a background of misunderstanding and hostility. In its new cultural milieu the radical memory often clashed with civic notions of honor and shame and the expectations of patronage and reciprocity (see Moxnes 1997).

The earliest Christian writings provide much evidence of the development of an urban embodiment of the Christian faith within the specific context of the Greco-Roman cities. The balance in early Christianity shifted quickly from the predominantly Jewish urban-village culture of Palestine to the cosmopolitan ports and colonies of the Mediterranean. This change took place in the midst of the rapid urbanization that has already been described. In Asia Minor and Achaia urban colonization had taken place because of the need to settle soldiers retiring from the army; these were joined by migrants from the outlying provinces of the Roman Empire. These would have been enhanced by groups of peripatetic artisans and hawkers who had followed the movements of the army and the usual mixed bag of merchants looking for suppliers and new markets. As ports, these cities were nodes in the communication and trade networks that crisscrossed the empire, eventually leading to Rome itself. The Imperial City was the center and rationale of the globalization project; the empire was its footprint from which it extracted its resources, material and human.

The new municipalities were to be meeting places for ethnic and religious diversity. Settlers found themselves alongside people who were different, and needed to develop new patterns of community life as they faced pluralistic and social challenges unknown in their countries of origin. This is the context against which scholars such as Wayne Meeks (1983) and Gerd Theissen (1983) put the expansion of the Christian movement under Paul and the other early missionaries. Meeks particularly portrays Paul as a city person, educated within the distinctive world of "urban Judaism," with the ability of an itinerant urban artisan to support himself (Meeks 1983, 9). Working in Greek, the *lingua franca* of the urban world movement, communication was made possible over a wide-ranging network of ports and other cities. Meeks comments that the variegated nature of life in these cities broke down many of the divisions and conventions of classical city life, giving urban existence a fluidity and excitement as well as "producing tensions and uncertainties" as manners, attitudes, and status were subverted (Meeks 1983, 16–20).The new Christian communities lived on these social fault lines:

> Urban society in the early Roman Empire was scarcely less complicated than our own, in proportion to the scale of knowledge available to the individual and of the demands made upon him. Its complexity—its untidiness to the mind—may well have been felt with special acuteness by people who were marginal or transient, either physically, socially or both, as so many identifiable members of the Pauline churches seem to have been. In any case, Paul and the other founders and leaders of those groups engaged aggressively in the creation of a new social reality. (Meeks 1983, 104)

In such places Paul established these new communities that crossed many of the usual divisions of class, ethnicity, and status but in its initial stages found its rooting particularly among the nonélite (Theissen 1983, 69).

> The ethos of the cities also contributed to the identity and self-understanding of these urban Christians. It is impossible to understand the significance of Paul's boast to "have become all things to all [people]" (1 Corinthians 9:22) outside the context of the pluralism of the Hellenistic city. Nor was this pluralism racial only. The controversies in the Corinthian groups over sexual practice, food taboos, idol worship, and hair-styles all bear witness to the "cultural potpourri" which influenced their style of life. (Barton 1987, 170)

The new Christian communities had counterparts in many of the small social, ethnic, and religious groups or associations found in those cities. These urban social forms, such as the assembly, *ekklesia,* and the household *(oikos)* were adapted in the forms and language of the Christian community (Meeks 1983, 31; Barton 1987, 169). Much has been written about the physical forms these communities took and the places in which they met. Like the Jewish communities of the Diaspora meeting as synagogues, the Christian assemblies met in whatever was the most convenient space available; with no particular halls set aside for such purposes, the gatherings would almost certainly have been in domestic surroundings. Early on, the church seems to have developed a cellular form based on families and households (Rom 16:5; 1 Cor 16:19) gathering in small cells throughout a city, coming together for a specific occasion or ritual (1 Cor 14:23). The courtyards and atriums of larger houses have been the preferred settings for many scholars describing these gatherings (see Murphy-O'Connor 1983, 161–68). First Corinthians 16:19 describes a group meeting in the home of artisan-tentmakers, Aquila and Prisca—maybe a workshop space on the ground floor of a four- or five-story tenement, large enough for about ten believers (Jewett 1994, chap. 6). Robert Jewett suggests that in Rome the evidence of a concentration of the oldest Christian sites in the Trastevere and

Porta Capena areas is a good indication as to the social makeup of those gatherings and the spaces they met in:

> Roman statistics indicate that Trastevere was the most densely populated section of the city with the highest proportion of high-rise slum dwellings in the city. . . . Trastevere was full of immigrants out of the East and was the site of mystery religions and temples. (Jewett 1994, 78)

Jewett also cites the names of the Roman Christian leaders, few of which are Latin, as evidence of a mostly immigrant lower-class and slave church. This challenges much received scholarship about the emergent church being solely reliant on patrons and modeling itself on secular hierarchical models. Later writing, such as the manual for church governance, written in Paul's name, understands congregational order in terms of the well-ordered middle-class household (1 Tim 2:9–15; 3:4–5) (Meeks 1983, 38–39), but that model cannot account for the variety of practices that seems apparent elsewhere in the epistles. The household *(oikos)* cannot be solely limited to the dwellings of the middle and upper classes but must include the homes and workshops of the slums in which a very different style of leadership would have emerged.

Despite the occasional collision of personal and cultural narratives, these groups succeeded in spreading some sense of corporate belonging and identity. Were the diverse and scattered early Christian communities "good news" for the poor and insecure who formed them? In his letters Paul often seems to challenge those who are attempting to structure the emergent communities along the standards and norms of the society in which they lived. Sergio Rostagno argues that the inclusion of the urban heathen poor is Paul "intuitively" realizing "the gospel event of the last becoming first" (Rostagno n.d., 36). *Ekklesia* is a crucial designation, drawn partly from the secular town meeting but maybe also with the solemn assemblies before Mount Sinai recorded in the *torah* in mind (Deut 9:10; Hebrew—*qahal,* Septuagint—*ekklesia*). At one level this has an ironic label, suggesting a significance out of all proportion to the social standing of those of which it was composed (overvalorization) (Meeks 1983, 45) yet at the same time a reminder of the expectations of the gathering in the purposes and practice of God's new order. Michel Clévenot similarly describes how Paul uses the term *ekklesia* as designating not "only a gathering but rather the specific practice of these communities articulated at the economic, political, and ideological levels as faith, hope and love" (Clévenot 1985, 127–28).

In such ways the diverse and scattered early Christian communities offered an alternative pattern of social interaction for those who encountered them. The excitement of the early church was that something new was happening among the urban landless masses of the Roman Empire. Though in political terms they were powerless, there was a discovery of a bond and a vision greater than those that dominated the culture and society of their cities. Young and Ford describe the experiences thus:

> The gospel is a proclamation of events and their central character; its transmission generates new events of suffering, conflict, foundation of communities, generosity, praise, prayer, and much else; and there is urgency about its communication which is powerfully productive of new history. (Young and Ford 1988, 240)

Beyond the local gathering, the connectivity, the network of Christian communities, underpinned the impact of the gospel. They began to reflect on, draw out, and implement the significance of the narratives and teachings they had come to know, not least working through the implications of the story of Jesus in the corporate lives of those it has touched. The Christian communities behind the earliest writings were interacting with the stories of the distant and recent past to discern what lifestyle they were being called to in the present and the possible futures that their newly acquired faith opened up for them.

It is not only in epistles and the descriptions of the early church in Acts that we encounter the first Christians attempting to deal with social division and scandal, in the light of its shared memory. From the work of the Gospel writers we glimpse a body of people striving to come to terms with, to make sense of its retelling of the stories of Jesus and that radical memory of God's new order, as social groupings interact within the church in a way that became notorious in the cities of that time.

In its new cultural milieu this memory often clashed with conventional notions of the patronage and reciprocity of the urban élites,[1] "ritualised and moralized dependence [that] fixed people in stable relationships with each other" (Meeks 1983, 40). As new communities, they were striving for a common identity. Mary Ann Beavis detects "Luke" retelling the story of Jesus, with a coherent theme of "marginalized" groups (Beavis 1997, 143), and goes on to suggest that it is a particularly Lukan contribution to Christian ethics to combine prophetic ideas of welfare with a critique of the rich in the call for a discipleship of equals: "he forges beyond the condemnation of the élite to a vision of a community of spiritual equals in which social disparities are vigorously and conscientiously addressed" (Beavis 1997, 150). It would have been this call to adopt a radical egalitarian stance that presented the greatest challenge to the readers of the Gospel who formed the new Christian communities against the patronage conventions of Hellenistic culture.

The diversity of content in the Gospel narratives and the epistles are an indication of the particularities of each author or editor's setting. The work of Michael Crosby identifies a similar process in the particular urban Christian community for which Matthew's Gospel was written. As the church in (probably) Antioch became more based on the households of those who were more educated, financially secure, and successful, "Matthew" emphasizes the need for justice within the household of God that would come about only through a radical reordering in the light of the history and perspectives that his story of Jesus assumes (Crosby 1988, 46–48). Wayne Meeks uses the phrase "Messianic Biography as Community forming Literature" (Meeks 1987, 136) to describe this approach of the Gospel writers. Rather than having Jesus as a sage or philosopher figure with an ethical system, the teachings of Jesus are recorded within a narrative that gives a framework that touches on Matthew's community's present experience and allows for an ethical response according to the contemporary situation:

> for all the church's inevitable retrojection of its experiences into the time of Jesus, this author does find ways to accord to the past an integrity of its own. It is not only a model for the present but also a basis which is different from the present and which therefore requires different responses. (Meeks 1987, 142–43)

> It is therefore possible to ask not only what *did* Jesus say, but what *does* he now wish his people to do—a sort of enquiry that obviously produced considerable dissension among the prophets and other leaders of the Matthean community. (Meeks 1987, 143)

The retelling of the Jesus narrative that comes out of that community reflects that community's common life and struggles as they went through a quite sophisticated hermeneutical process in their particular location. It is the narrative that filters their individual and corporate narratives, alongside those which they receive as "Scripture."

The Possibility of Community

So how did the first urban Christians handle the narratives of previous marginal communities? In Paul's letters and the Letter to the Hebrews, Abraham is claimed as a model of faith and the key to a theology of promise for a new minority community that relies on hope and faith despite the evidence to the contrary around them. Their presence in the cities of the Roman world is a sign that God is still calling communities into being and proving faithful to them. In a first-century urban setting there is no "prosperity theology" based on Abraham's great wealth or his social status alongside kings or nomadic warlords;[2] rather, in his discussion of the significance of Abraham, Paul writes of him living out his faith in the presence of God, who "gives life to the dead and calls into existence the things that do not exist" (Rom 4:17). Paul is calling the Roman Christians "to do good things within the framework of trust in God who bases his promises on grace . . . [who] . . . calls into existence a fellowship which before did not exist" (Achtemeier 1985, 83). As Paul negotiates a place for outsiders in the purposes of God, a radical vision is renewed as the outsider, landless ancestor is claimed. In the promise lies the possibility that things can be different, a promise already demonstrated in the resurrection event. God's new order is apparent for those who would perceive them in the struggles and the new community of relationships that has been called into being. This theme is picked up, later, when the author of the Letter to the Hebrews recites the ancestry of faith for a community living on the edge. A common belief becomes apparent, located in the possibility of a new order that they had glimpsed in their community life. As they find themselves excluded from participation in the civic realm, marginal in an urban society that they are unable to comprehend fully, they look for a place where strangers and exiles are at home, "the city that has foundations, whose architect and builder is God" (Heb 11:10).

Urban Disclosure

It is that emergent ambivalence, the ethos of which seems so at variance with Jeremiah's instructions to the exiles, that develops into the antipathy toward the imperial urban order that we find in John's Revelation. The diatribe against the city in Rev 18 is an attack on the urban culture to which the struggling Christian communities found themselves so opposed. The cities and towns of Asia Minor and the imperial urban culture of Rome, which they imitated so closely, are brought to book by the evil that was ingrained so deeply in the edifice of Roman power. The Christian communities that the seer addresses are challenged about the reality of a civic culture that has recently been responsible for the persecution of their fellow believers. The cults of the imperial family and the divine personification of Rome, around which so much of civic life was based, are the symbolic manifestations of an economic system based on "inhuman brutality [and] contempt for human life" (Bauckham 1991, 79).

Echoing the dirges of the Old Testament prophets, the seer begins by attacking the mercantile life of the city, an economy built on luxury goods and the abuse of human dignity (Rosing 1999, chaps. 1, 4). The desolation of the city is an act of judgment on a culture that perpetuates the myth of the trickle-down effect of wealth creation, of social stability through bread and circuses, of the overvalorization of a single insatiable city site at the heart of an idolatrous empire. The church is called out of the city, to set itself apart from the structures of sin and the coming judgment. This is not so much a geographical relocation but a reorientation within, of Christians' social location within the culture of the urban communities where the hearers-readers are situated. Leonard Thompson describes Revelation as "a minority report on how Christians relate to the larger Roman society. The seer is apparently advocating attitudes and styles of life not compatible with how most Christians were living in the cities of Asia" (Thompson 1990, 132). There is a suggestion that those Christians who have assimilated (those condemned in the earlier letters to the churches of the seven cities in Asia Minor), who have enjoyed the luxuries of the city, will be brought up with a jolt when they find themselves mourning alongside the key economic stakeholders of Babylon (Bauckham 1991). At a safe distance the community of God can watch the ruins smolder.

John's Revelation is based on a succession of counterimages. Those who have distanced themselves from the culture of Babylon behold an invitation to participate in a new urban order, not based on the strata of patronage and trade but on practice of the divine presence. The city is portrayed as reward for those who have endured, who have proved faithful through the testings and persecutions of urban life. Yet it is no village for the faithful few but a vast place at which one can only wonder at its inclusivity in geopolitical terms (Rev 22:2) and its maintenance through the ceaseless activities of just service (Rev 22:3) and governance (Rev 22:5). The possibility to enter that new order is left to the reader to accept or decline, according to their response in the community they are part of, now (see Royalty 1998; Boring 1989, 216–24).

Using the Canon of Urban Experience

To conclude this account of the biblical experience of the urban environment with Revelation may leave the reader wondering "What then?" or "So what?" We cannot expect a blueprint for the ordering of urban life or, for that matter, of urban Christian discipleship. While Scripture may at times be ambivalent or derogative about urban structures it never advocates physical withdrawal from urban space. What does become apparent, however, is that the record of faith does show how the people of God have responded to the urban environment and its wider socioeconomic context and how that encounter has been a contributing factor in the experience and understanding of community and faith. At the same time there is the abiding conviction that they should not accept the ordering environment or its culture as nonnegotiable. Stephen Sykes has written, "The biblical portrait of the Church, warts and all, remains foundational in the capacity to inform the minds of those who continue to discern the Church's way in new circumstances" (Sykes 1995, 131).

For a community to imagine itself as the people of God in a particular historical context, in the midst of the social forces that have been described in the first-century Mediterranean world or the globalizing, urbanizing world of the twenty-first century, is a defiant countercultural act that connects with "and embodies the essential narrative reference characterising the raw material of all Christian theology. Ecclesiology has always to be related to the specific experience of a concrete people in history, acting within the context of the covenant of God" (Sykes 1995, 129). This approach is paralleled in the ecclesiology of liberation theologian Leonardo Boff, who insists that "[the people of God] is not a formal concept devoid of historical materiality. It seeks to be a real and not metaphorical designation of the Church; but for it to be a real designation there has to be the real historical existence of a people which through its organising itself in its Christian faith emerges as the People of God" (Boff 1985, 93).

Marianne Sawicki develops this through an interpretation of archaeological and Gospel evidence that finds a resistive political praxis (being salt and yeast, rather than assuming an imminent exodus-style liberation) in what she calls the "paleochurch"—the earliest forms the church took in Palestine and Syria:

> It seems preferable to take with utmost seriousness the findings of historical scholarship, especially the finding that the paleochurch accommodated the words and practices of Jesus to the urban spaces of the empire. The paleochurch understood itself to be achieving solidarity and continuity with Jesus while adapting its activities to the evolving challenges of imperial colonization after Calvary. It achieved persistence amid historical change. What continued after Calvary was Jesus' refusal of the totalitarian claims of the empire that world markets and steeply stratified social classes were the best and only way to organize life on earth. . . . The way of salt and leaven is not absolutely authoritative; it is relatively authoritative insofar as churches today encounter circumstances like those in occupied Palestine. (Sawicki 2000, 175)

The imagination of faith refuses to be content with human arrangements—social, economic, political, urban, rural—that are not based on the practice of human freedom in the presence of God. That imagination will pertinently challenge those arrangements through envisioning alternatives, through prophetic speech and action, through the creation of communities that include, strengthen, and give integrity to those at the margins. A parallel might be drawn with the potency of African American subversive historiography, which according to bell hooks:

> connects oppositional practices from the past and forms of resistance in the present, thus creating spaces of possibility where the future can be imagined differently—imagined in a way that we can witness ourselves dreaming, moving forward and beyond the limits of confines of fixed locations. (quoted in Sandercock 1998, 1)

In the following chapters I want to examine the shape of the church that might be imagined in the midst of the urban currents of our world in the near future.

Notes

1. "Their life centred on a meal that served as a means of integration, not just of Jews and non-Jews but also of members from various status groups and social positions. The ethos of the meal represented a break with the city ideals of patronage, benefactions, and the quest for honour. It is not unthinkable that such criticism of city ideals could also have been aimed at community members from the 'elite periphery' " (Moxnes 1997, 174).

2. In his commentary on Genesis, Brueggemann makes the comment that it is only recent scholarship that has portrayed Abraham as a nomadic prince (Brueggemann 1982, 110).

Part Three

Patterns and Models for a Church in an Urban World

Chapter Eight

Being Church—Between Local and Global

Locating Presence and Engagement

The church in all its forms finds itself enmeshed in the multiple layers of difference and distance that are to be encountered in global urban society. This is the greatest challenge that faces our theology as it negotiates and speaks alongside and within the diverse, competing, conflicting cultural claims on the future. What then might it mean for local pastoral praxis to be also global political praxis? To live real presence through communities that include, strengthen, and give integrity to those who live in the margins of our urban society?

The Catholic writer Robert Schreiter considers addressing these challenges to be a primary task, particularly in the creation of a theology that engages with these changes in Europe. The future which that theology struggles for must involve an equitable access to the basic means of human life—housing, employment, education, medical care—accompanied by recognition of diversity, respect of difference, and the creation of meeting points for cooperation and communication (Schreiter 1997, 94–95). Like Leonie Sandercock, he considers the lucidity of process to be a key factor—"theology must in all forms be intelligible to its communities, but also in forms commensurate with how meaning is being shaped in contemporary society" (Schreiter 1997, 97). To be appropriate to the new locally diverse and globally connected society that is emerging, theology must develop a base that includes among its tasks the creation of "a utopian horizon for cultural inclusion and transformation" (Schreiter 1997, 97).

Although not directly addressing the issues of urban settlements, Schreiter's challenge is to engage with the processes, movements, and policy trends that are shaping national and regional futures: to bring into the communal arena a vision that goes beyond self-interest, that advocates those who have no voice at the location of power, a vision drawn from the negotiated and remolded space of urban communities. One area where this is vital is in the contested arena of regeneration initiatives, a critical arena for engagement. Such initiatives are often not the good news for the poor, particularly those from excluded minorities, they claim to be but are rather orientated to the needs of local governments and professionals engaged in the programs. Similar things may be said about other initiatives—local, regional, national, or global, based on the rhetoric of economic or social development. Imagining a different city, a different future will mean that we have to engage with the epistemological assumptions of those who are in the vanguard of urban and social policy (see Amin, Massey, and Thrift 2000).

As we have seen, urban experience and process affect all elements of life—social, cultural, and political; this is usually concurrent with movements of resistance and transformation, the significance of which should not be underplayed. The persistence of faith communities in what many urbanologists have assumed to be a secular urban landscape forces the questions about how such communities adapt to and resist different elements of the urban experience. The tensions people experience in urban life throw them between the roles of object and subject in a manner that may leave them seemingly alienated and exhausted, unable to participate in shaping the human and built domains as arenas for justice.

Urban or Suburban

What type of community is the church we find in urban areas? How do the trends of wider church life impact on the vision for the church described above? To answer this, I want to explore a little how the church looks within the UK urban landscape.

Just as our urban communities are caught up in processes and change on an unprecedented scale, we witness the Christian faith responding and changing in the context of new challenges and opportunities. The church is part of the urban scene. As a voluntary institution it finds itself alongside social welfare, organizing groups, and other faith communities as subject to changing trends in participation apparent in all parts of civil society. In poor urban areas, faith is prevalent in the private and public realm, often more openly acknowledged in poorer communities; those areas with significant immigrant populations account for some of the higher rates of religious activity. The private, however, seems to dominate, with church attendance on a plateau or in decline, while prayer and belief become private concerns with little need for a corporate expression. These trends alongside the growth of individualistic New Age therapies and practices have been defined by one British sociologist as "believing without belonging" (Davie 1994). Historian Adrian Hastings notes, "Whatever happens to the churches in England in the twenty-first century, they have already become a minority constituency within the nation as a whole, although there remains a fairly large penumbra of sympathy beyond the bonds of any formal commitment" (Hastings 2001, lviii).

"Believing without belonging" is paralleled in the voluntary activities that make up civil society. Robert Putnam has written of how, in the United States, more people are using bowling alleys, which are springing up as part of out-of-town shopping and leisure complexes, yet few will join a bowling club or league. For Putnam, this indicates shrinking "social capital"—the community-building capacity on which societies draw (Putnam 2000). The churches are very much part of that social capital ledger. In church life, skills develop, as well as beliefs and ideals, and this has implications for charitable giving as well as engagement in wider community issues. The extent to which that engagement takes place is dependent on the churches' prevailing theology:

church attendance is both correlated with membership and indeed leadership in secular groups. In both evangelical and mainline congregations, the religiously involved learn transferable civic skills, such as management and public speaking, but mainline Protestants are more likely to transfer them to the wider community. (Putnam 2000, 78)

In Britain there is a growing social engagement among evangelicals engaged in urban mission and ministry, and the concerns of this book will not be new for many of them (though many find the transition from social welfare provisions to being advocates for social justice a difficult one to make). For the most part, these are evangelicals who are culturally aware of the dangers of confusing faith and suburban culture. The shift which is a concern is that it is in the suburbs, in churches practicing a particularly individualistic form of faith, that there are signs of numerical growth and increasing influence in national church life. Though suburban values are not confined to one style or tradition of church, these would be characterized by an unwillingness to associate issues of faith with social justice or an inclusive worldview.

The suburban church does not organize as an explicit group within church politics, but its interests are served by the failure of the church to take seriously the reality of structural sin and the challenges of social analysis to its corporate life. Sociologist Anthony Giddens defines power as "the transformative capacity of human action" (Giddens 1994, 117)—a key concept in understanding the control of the process of change. Any society or social group (this will include churches) will find unequally distributed levels of influence over the processes by which the rules and resources that shape that social group are changed or transformed. Those holding power will mold that community's life according to how their sectional interests are best served, thus enhancing and legitimating their position with little regard for those unable to initiate change. These actions may be unconscious or unintended. They are, however, the inevitable outcome of the initial uneven distribution of power.

The dominance of suburban Christianity in the historic denominations in Britain and North America[1] is apparent in the promotion of activities, policies, and programs that meet its sectional interests. These will often use the rhetoric of transformation and change but will ignore or fail to promote critical reflection on wider issues of lifestyle, social responsibility, or power. This has been particularly apparent in programs identified over the past decade with evangelism, church growth, and catechesis. For example, the Alpha Course, originating in an affluent church in London's West-End , has advanced forms of primary catechetics from a charismatic base. Through effective marketing it has become a brand rather than a model, dominating church life. Adherence to the structure and full content of the course is stressed if the integrity of brand is to be honored. The course offers little scope for critical interaction with the material presented (with a notably selective use of Scripture) or with the systems of injustice in which the participants are caught through their work or social location. There is no opportunity to analyze the impact of current practices in financial markets or the consumption aspects of suburban lifestyles; cultural inclusion and social transformation are not considered as part of the gospel mandate or baptismal covenant. All in all, the process of the course assumes a social and cultural base for church life that is remote from the urban experience in poor urban areas. Many churches are in danger of becoming the spiritual equivalents of gated communities, where, in the words of novelist J. G. Ballard "The most educated, creative and able people, in whom society has invested a great deal are going to step outside society and lock the door" (quoted in Hari 2001).

These cultural divides are nowhere more apparent than when the obligation to presence in every community is not part of the church's mandate. Writing from New York Peter Marcuse identifies the key signs of change for those mapping exclusion and division among the city's varied population. A Starbucks Coffeehouse will indicate an area "on the up";

different recreational and religious facilities will mark an area's social composition:

> Jockey clubs will be in the luxury city, country clubs in the gentrified city, baseball fields in the suburban city, basketball courts in the tenement city, fire hydrants in the abandoned city. And divided locational practices similarly characterize religious institutions, from storefront evangelical sects in the abandoned city to high Episcopalian in the luxury city. (Marcuse 2000, 277)

For Christians in poor urban communities, access to power is limited, not just because of their reluctance to participate in the quasi-democratic structures of the church but because of the ability of dominant groups to maintain processes and language that are inaccessible to those who have been excluded. The dominant will be deluded if they think that because the structures are supposedly democratic they are accessible to everyone. Surveying the social makeup of the General Synod of the Church of England, eight year safter the influential *Faith in the City* report, Grace Davie commented:

> There is . . . no getting away from the fact that the House of Laity remains essentially a middle-class body, filled with well-educated individuals who are prepared and able to offer a great deal to the Church in the form of talents and time. . . .

> General Synod can be an intimidating place in which both experience and expertise are necessary for survival. And it is bound to attract a certain type of individual, one all too easy to stereotype. Such individuals are not necessarily unrepresentative of churchgoing opinion even if they fall short of a perfect microcosm. (Davie 1994, 170)

The language of liturgy, church growth models, ministerial formation, and assumptions about lifestyle all remain suburban. If, as Nicholas Lash proposes, "the fundamental form of the Christian interpretation of scripture is the life, activity and organisation of the believing community" (Lash 1986, 43) this is a situation that needs to be addressed, not least by an alternative approach to Scripture and Christian nurture.

The suburban church cannot, however, be written off; or rather, the communal life of Christians in suburban areas must be challenged. Whatever changes happen in our urban areas over the coming years, people will continue to live in suburbs—what is vital is that the Christian community comes to understand its presence in all parts of the city as being the foundation for the radical transformation of all levels and forms of urban living. At the same time, smallness—which is a characteristic of most churches outside the suburban model—should not be considered solely in negative terms; Sawicki's use of the salt and leaven metaphors comes to mind. This could be seen as an imperative to challenge the proliferation of the "Mega Church" model which takes discipleship (by automobile) out of its spatial particularity and locatedness into "high-production, high-entertainment" culture of the church as mall—a neutral, privatized environment with minimized opportunities for risk, encounter, or participation. (See Leong 2001, 299–303.) Sawicki takes her metaphors further, as the essential basis for resistance to the colonization of images of the lives of Christians by the ideologies of consumerism and suburbanism:

> resistance . . . can take the form of small scale refusals to comply with the alleged inevitability of the pomps and glamours of middle class life. Among I would name: automobiles and the commuting lifestyle . . . fashionable clothing manufactured offshore under oppressive labor conditions; the subtle self replicating practices of racism and classism. . . . The Kingdom of God is sought resistively. (Sawicki 2000, 79)

Even the social capital approach of Robert Putnam does not offer a critical account of the nature of the community to which those activities are contributing or their ecological impact. (See Budde and Brimlow 2000.)

Survival, faithfulness, and renewal do, however, depend on the church's ability to change and connect in new ways within the urban, global context of which it is part. In an otherwise disappointing review of the social care projects in the capital, the Bishop of London provided some insight into the potential of these communities in an essay concerning ministry:

> The Christian task is to renew the local eucharistic communities which already exist in their thousands. Too many of them at present are aggregations of people who, in a parody of the consumerist culture around them, regard the Church as an institution which ought to cater for their religious needs and feelings. Real conversion involves a passage from a consumer-style Christianity, where most of us naturally started, to a sense of Christian citizenship in which everyone of the faithful understands what God is calling them to be and do in order to build the future of Jesus Christ. . . . It ought not to be possible to pray "thy kingdom come" without appreciating the cost in terms of personal commitment. (Chartres 1995, 40)

The ideologies that manipulate the church will often deny the possibility of critical engagement with or transformation of institutional bias, oppression, or institutional forms of racism. Giddens describes ideology as the means through which dominant groups maintain control, portraying their sectional interests as universal (Giddens 1979, 6), a process that Edward Schillebeeckx recognizes all too readily in the Catholic Church: "the institutional church has had a tendency to universalize precisely its non-universal, historically inherited, particular features tied up with a particular culture and time and apply them uniformly to the whole of the Catholic world" (Schillebeeckx 1990, 167–68).

The challenge we face in the large cities throughout North America and Europe is: to what extent are we prepared to let the detrimental urban forms and social trends we see around us be reproduced in the lives of our churches? Congregations, city-wide church life, and denominational networks all have tendencies to accept certain aspects of context as inevitable in their own lives; this can lead to an unquestioning compliance with those trends—gentrification, segregation, white-flight economic polarization, the increasing exclusion of minorities, or the delocalization of concerns leading to indifference to the weakening of democratic institutions. In the next chapter I want to explore an alternative model of catholicity that can inform and reshape the church for its calling in a globalizing, urbanizing world, but first I want to examine another aspect of how urban church life is changing and the complexities which the church encounters within itself.

Global Flows and the Church amid Minority Ethnic Communities

The global socioeconomic flows affecting the population of the global city have also changed the broader religious landscape in recent decades, adding religious diversity to the layers of contestation. Minority ethnic churches make up a significant proportion of Christian communities in British cities, particularly those with African-Caribbean and African communities based on waves of immigration during the 1950s–1960s and 1980s–1990s respectively. They are probably the best-organized part of the voluntary sector within the black community. They are certainly the location of the majority of black voluntary giving, but they have not yet the confident identity of African American churches. Despite their context, these churches are not self-consciously urban churches—that is, part of wider urban mission networks or pursuing an urban contextual analysis; they are, however, developing significant social ministries and beginning to engage ecumenically with local authorities. In global terms there are significant transnational flows of personnel and resources.

The social and economic difficulties, or the often violent racism faced by their members, have not led to an explicit militancy or black theology. Again exceptions are emerging, apparent particularly in the work of second-generation black Christians, notably Birmingham-based theologian Robert Beckford (Beckford 1998; 2000; 2001). Minority ethnic churches often provide a security and support structure that mainstream denominations have been unable to offer because of competing interests within the local church. Grace

Davie develops this point when she comments in her survey of postwar British religion:

> For many black congregations, the sense of community grows out of the church which is its principal reason for existence. In contrast, a traditional English church—and the Church of England is the most obvious example—forms a religious focus within a given community for those who wish to take up its services (in both senses of the term), bearing in mind that there are very many ways in which this take-up may be effected. (Davie 1994, 112)

Although worship may be seen, or rather preached, as primary in these churches (see Edwards 1992) their sociological role within ethnic communities suggests that they often act as religious foci within given networks. Although proclaiming a universal gospel, it is often unacknowledged that African-Caribbean and West African churches tend to draw the majority of their members from single ethnic or regional groups. The given geographical communities within which the historic denominations operate is very different from the wider, cross-city networks that are drawn together in minority ethnic churches. An American observer of the black British scene commented in the 1980s: "The joining of a Pentecostal church is not just dropping out of Anglican culture, but it is the search for a place conducive to the nurturing of a cultural system which will not be dominated or repressed" (Evans 1985, 63).

This is a very different situation to the historic black churches in North America. A closer parallel might be drawn in the experience of more recent waves of immigration and the struggle by the Hispanic American community and others to establish their cultural identity, within the Roman Catholic Church as well as a new presence within Protestant denominations. Eldin Villafañe sees the growth of a Hispanic Pentecostal Church as a struggle for "a place of cultural survival and affirmation" (Villafañe 1995, 32) among one of the most socially disadvantaged groups.

The growth of minority ethnic churches in Britain is a sign of their ability to tap into communities that transcend local geographical contexts (with members often crossing cities to attend) as immigrants search for a place of identity and belonging alongside their faith journey. The cold welcome received by black Anglicans, Methodists, and others in their mother churches during the 1950s and 1960s is well documented (see Leech 1988; Wilkinson 1994). To be told that one doesn't belong in the church that claims to be the church for your locality will often send one into communities and networks that make no geographical claim. The resilience of some black Anglicans who have stuck with their church despite everything is stunning. They are very definite as to why the Pentecostal option was inappropriate for them, even though there is much in these churches that resonates at an innate subjective level.

More recently, Lorraine Dixon has written of her spiritual journey and struggle for self-awareness as a British-born black woman in a predominantly white denomination: "I had to leave anything that gave me a sense of myself as a black person at the church door and engage with worship that did not value diversity or cultural difference. . . . The Church I belonged to, did not provide a space either in its liturgical or social life for . . . self-discovery" (Dixon 2000, 25–26). Dixon describes how that self-identity developed through the license to name the elements of a black spiritual heritage and engage with other strands of that tradition as well as those who have fought to make black people visible in the theological and iconographic life of the church. It is a story of negotiation but not compromise; of crossing borders and networking, sustained by the belief that transformation is possible. "The sacrament of black presence has sought to herald a realized vision of freedom, equity and real change for all" (Dixon 2000, 37).

Writing of a similar situation (i.e., being a Hispanic congregation in a predominantly Anglo denomination), where language accompanies cultural affirmation, Teresa Chávez Sauceda comments:

> Hispanic congregations see themselves as something more than a non-English-speaking Presbyterian church, more than being

> merely a menas to an end, a way station for the culturally
> unassimilated. . . . the use of language in worship has served
> to bring about a clearer recognition of the degree to which
> Hispanic Presbyterians value their Hispanic heritage and desire
> to express their faith, to praise and to pray to god in ways that
> reflect who they are as a people, rather than to adopt exclusively
> the forms and symbols of another people and culture. (Chávez
> Sauceda 1996, 93)

It is Christians from minority ethnic communities who
are responsible for the persistence of life in the historic
denominations in the major cities, particularly in poor neighborhoods—a fact often unacknowledged by the historic denominations, which would do well to bear in mind Justo
González's words concerning the Hispanic Christian community within the Episcopal Church in New York: "What all
this means is that when we understand the significance of
the poor for the proper understanding of Scripture and of the
Christian faith, we must come to the conclusion that a
church that does not have the poor in its midst, a church that
does not identify with the poor, is at a decided disadvantage"
(quoted in Villafañe 1995, 36).

The situations being described are changing rapidly. In
Britain most commentators on the experience of black Anglicans writing during recent decades have described primarily
the African-Caribbean experience, emphasizing the political
nature of "blackness"—the common experience of racism
and social exclusion was considered to give the nonwhite
community a common identity (Evans 1985, 58; see also
Wilkinson 1994). Recent studies suggest that this ideological solidarity is becoming increasingly harder to maintain
as ethnic communities display very different levels of self-
identity as well as achievement (particularly educational)
and disadvantage (see Modood et al. 1997). Similarly, few
commentators have taken into account the large influx, particularly in London, of West Africans and other groups. (The
same is true with research on Islam, which has an increasing
West African constituency in these areas.) There is also a
notable movement between Christianity and Islam among

African and African-Caribbean people. New migrant communities and evangelistic work within them are shifting the minority ethnic profile of both faiths.[2]

These new influxes also affect the historic denominations, which find themselves in a new situation of greater diversity and a very different set of congregational dynamics. Churches become communities where contestation, resistance, and negotiation are everyday realities (see Beckford 1998, 42–60). The greater diversity will not just be cultural but will also include expectations of levels of participation and education, as well as identity and gender issues. A local church seeking to include such diversity, when there are numerous pressures on its members from outside anxieties and ties, must discover a sense of identity and community that can hold seemingly conflicting interests together. The institutional racism, identified in the London Metropolitan Police by the report into the circumstances surrounding the investigation of the murder of black teenager Stephen Lawrence (Macpherson 1999), is still a significant factor preventing full participation by minority ethnic people in the life of the historic denominations and in many parts of civil society. The embodiment of diversity is becoming a particularly important aspect of being church in marginal, as well as some better-off, communities. The cultural affirmation will be a patient process of encouragement, of listening, and of sharing the contribution and insight that each brings. Faramelli, Rodman, and Scheibner detect a need to look at the assumptions that lie behind theological education and vocational development in the Episcopal Church in the United States, as it responds to recent waves of Hispanic and Asian migration:

> The prospects for ministering to new people are hampered by the still prevalent suburban mentality, and the fact that most seminary graduates are more prepared for a suburban parish than any other kind of ministry. . . . given the new ethnic and racial groupings in our cities, the Episcopal Church is not adequately training a new generation of clergy leadership. In a word, the Episcopal Church has yet to deal with the issue of inclusivity and the realities of a multicultural and multiracial world.(Faramelli, Rodman, and Scheibner, 119)

What are the implications of globalization for ministry in these communities? What are the challenges which our institutions and programs for ministerial formation need to meet? In chapter 10 responses to these new situations which have led to new ministries of organizing, advocacy, or enabling will be described. Yet even traditional pastoral ministries can present new challenges within ethnically diverse congregations. Instant travel and communication will have an impact on how people whose families live in other countries behave in times of crisis. Cross-border movements and exchange are part of everyday life, usually, but not always, negotiated with ease. For example, a telephone call will inform one of a family crisis demanding an instant response about travel, regardless of funds available; attendance at a funeral on another continent will be expected rather than attendance at a later memorial service. Different members of the same community will have different abilities to access travel and communication according to age, income, savings, and so on. Solidarity and assistance within the Christian community at such times is vital.

A diversity of cultures within a congregation often leads to fresh understandings of the role of narrative and the practice of community, as personal stories of migration and pilgrimage are retold against the backdrop of the biblical story (see Davey 1995). Personal links with churches in other countries offer a sharper understanding for whole congregations of issues previously considered remote. The stories and experiences of such congregations are vital to share as testimony of the "new opportunities" for reshaping communities for justice in the global city.

Notes

1. In Britain that is the Church of England, Methodism, Baptists, and the United Reformed Church. The Roman Catholic Church would normally be included in this category in Britain but has a very different history and social profile in relation to its presence in urban areas.

2. One of the best-documented areas is the London Borough of Newham. The third edition of the *Newham Directory of Religious Groups* (Aston Charities Trust 1999) lists over three hundred organizations, including Christians worshiping in Arabic, French, Coptic, Chinese, Amharic, Malayalam, Urdu, Punjabi, Spanish, and Twi. For a commentary by the directory compiler see Smith 1996.

For a wide-ranging collection of analyses of religious diversity and change in New York see Carnes and Karpathakis 2001.

Chapter Nine

Being Church—Between Presence and Flows

Networking Catholicity

In a world that is globalizing and urbanizing, identifying how local pastoral praxis is the other side of global political praxis is the process through which the church might rediscover its *catholicity*. Catholicity enables the church to offer an alternative paradigm to the tendencies of globalization to homogenization, power imbalances, and exclusion. At the same time, some aspects of globalization should be exploited to extend the church's capacity to be truly catholic, particularly amid the transnational flows of contemporary urban life.

Just as the local church may experience contestation and need to instigate careful negotiation within its communal life, the church in its global life will find that cultures, capabilities, and interests clash and connect at a number of different levels. Churches often find their global agendas dominated by the agendas that negotiate the contradictions between calls for uniformity in terms of doctrine and ethics and the reality of diversity at a local or regional level. These agendas are often introverted, taking the internal life of the church as context, detached from the realities of the forces reshaping the world at the many levels and frontiers on which the church is called to engage. Similarly, as has been noted in the earlier discussion of Manuel Castells, the presence of the church alongside and within the activities that are globalization is not always helped by the rigid hierarchical structures of its internal life.

✳   Catholicity is the dynamic attribute that enables the church to exist in tension within the local and the global. Like certain aspects of globalization, catholicity is about communication, not for its own sake but enabling enriching interaction and negotiation to take place. The local life of the church cannot exist in isolation—while responding to local conditions, the local church is informed, empowered, and supported by other localities and meeting points within the wider mesh of relationships that is the church. Robert Schreiter writes of a "new catholicity . . . marked by a wholeness of inclusion and fullness of faith in a pattern of intercultural exchange and communication" (Schreiter 1997, 132). Catholicity is kept alive by the sending and receipt of news; by the sharing of resources and models of practice; by people visiting other sites—as guests and friends, or in more formal exchanges of personnel; by including other perspectives in dialogue, decision making, and planning, through consciousness raising that provokes acts of advocacy and solidarity.

Catholicity is also about authenticity—the church being authentic to its calling in practice, wherever it is. *Orthopraxis* (right action) is thus closely allied with the evidence of orthodoxy (right belief). The local church is the vital presence that enables engagement in the reality of the lives and struggles of people and communities. Leonardo Boff takes this further: "The catholicity of the Church is the power to be incarnated, without losing its identity, in the most diverse cultures. To be catholic is not to simply expand the ecclesiastical system but to live and witness to the same faith in Jesus Christ, saviour and liberator, within a particular culture" (Boff 1985, 98).

The catholicity of a particular church, or movement of ✱ churches, is not manifested in its ordained ministry, liturgy, or hierarchy but in its faithfulness to its incarnational presence, its openness and its solidarity *(koinonia)* with the global Christian presence, its determination to be part of the ongoing reconciling work of God in Christ. Thus, in many ways, catholicity has much in common with Leonie Sandercock's *Cosmopolis,* being always in the making, a process of becoming, of envisioning possibility. Philip Sheldrake writes:

> The dynamism of catholicity pushes us forever to transgress boundaries and exceed limits. Catholic place, in our contingent experience, can never be simply an arrival point but always implies a future departure. This is because catholicity does not mean simply what is ubiquitous but what is whole and complete. (Sheldrake 2000, 70)

In many respects catholicity is a *global* practice—a homogeneous global church is a fallacy that puts the genuine incarnational task of the church at risk. For liberation theologians catholicity can no longer be expressed from the center but is rediscovered as a mutuality *(koinonia)* among diverse equals in solidarity with those traditionally at the periphery of the church and global society (Sobrino 1985, 110–11). For Jürgen Moltmann, that task lies in the church's commitment as a community to a common cause: its mission in the world, as it seeks the justice of the kingdom of God universally, for everyone. That wholeness and commonality must not, however, be confused with uniformity or neutrality: "The Church is related to the whole and is catholic in so far as, in the fragmentation of the whole, it primarily seeks and restores to favour the lost, the rejected and the oppressed" (Moltmann 1977, 352).

The *global* reality of the church poses challenges to some of the assumed patterns of engagement. The local presence cannot be parochial in the general sense and, more specifically, the way the local church is structured—"the parish model" may relate inadequately to the multifocused nature of contemporary urban life (see Shanks 1995). Reimagining current models will involve sensitivity and tenacity, alongside well-researched analysis of the connections, networks, and movements already touching or present in the local Christian community.

Koinonia—a New Solidarity?

In solidarity the church stands with those in whom it finds its vocation and alongside those in other places who share that calling. It is quite difficult to find a single English word to translate the Greek word *koinonia*. In the New Testament, the *koinos* group of words is used to denote the ideas of common life and sharing (Kittel and Friedrich 1985, 447–50). "Mutuality" or "solidarity" seem more appropriate translations than "fellowship" or "communion." *Koinonia* is a sharing, experiencing, and cooperating through which a common bond is attained with Christ and with other believers; it is the common condition of Christians that all are called to share (1 Cor 1:9). *Koinonia* is glimpsed in the life of the community (Phil 1:5), particularly in the celebration of the Lord's Supper (1 Cor 10) and in the living out of the gospel. *Koinonia* is not synonymous with *church*. Its presence is a sign of the church's faithfulness to mutuality and conviviality—the dynamic of relationships that builds up the whole body. It is what binds the local Christian presence with presences in other places, across the city and across the world. For Paul, the collection for the poor Christians in Palestine was a sign of that wider *koinonia* (Rom 15:26) as resources are shared not through altruism but awareness that other parts of the same body are suffering. In 2 Corinthians Paul considers this a dynamic mutuality within what was then the global network of Christian community, the embodiment of the hopes and longings of God's new order (2 Cor 8:4; 9:13). David Ford identifies the implications of this for contemporary Christian praxis: "The Church is expressed in terms of mutuality, coinheritance, communication, jointness and service. It is this which is most subversive yet also full of possibilities for the church and sociality today" (Ford 1989, 244). There is then a possibility of understanding the potential for the church as being the creation and sustaining of a "spirituality of mutuality" within physical localities, as well as the space of flows that is the medium of global processes.

Sacralizing and Connecting Place

A crucial way in which catholicity and *koinonia* are expressed is through the worship and the sacraments of the church. These are crucial activities that inform and enhance the whole life of the church in the particular geographical places that faith is incarnated. As a countercultural activity, liturgy becomes the means through which Christians stake their interest in a place by creating events, new histories— concrete, historicized acts that proclaim God's new order. In these terms the church becomes a sacramental presence: sacralizing space as an arena for the presence of justice, not in an exclusive "holy of holies" sense; as well as proclaiming the possibility of radical reordering of resources.

In his Anglican ecclesiology, Stephen Sykes expresses this in terms that anyone who has attempted to invigorate worship in urban churches can recognize: setting the worship in the specific context where the church is called to faithfulness. "Would it not be consistent with the Anglican tradition to see our churches offering on behalf of a specific part of the world which God loves the praise which it has forgotten to express?" (Sykes 1995, 203). Through worship, that should include engagement with Scripture, with possibilities being opened and explored; the imagination of God's new order breaking in creates a place in which justice must be practiced and from which the struggle for spatial justice must emanate. David Ford and Alistair McFadyen describe this process as the future being "praised open":

> Praise opens up the horizon within which present conditions can be seen to contradict the life and will of God; it energizes commitment to a new future, and it helps set an agenda for change. . . . There is the vocation of the Church to be a sanctuary of transformation. (Ford and McFadyen 1995, 98)

The renewal of worship in the urban church is an essential part of the Christian task in "a specific part of the world which God loves" and to which, some would say, God displays some kind of preferential option. It is worth emphasizing that worship in urban churches is not just about what happens within the four walls of a building on a Sunday morning for an hour; it is about what is offered by individuals and groups of friends and neighbors meeting in each other's apartments and houses for Eucharist, prayer, or a home blessing; about churches taking worship onto the street and into the parks during Holy Week and Easter and at times of community celebration and mourning; about sacralizing place through prayer walks; about churches joining together to engage with wider issues during One World Week or taking their worship onto the street in an act of witness or solidarity with groups working on humans rights or global economic justice. What does it mean for the *via dolorosa* to be actualized by a congregation on streets and public places which are being colonized by drug dealers, real-estate speculation, or CCTV cameras?

As observed in the previous chapter, what happens in particular urban parts of the world should, however, be watched, celebrated, and learned from by those in the non-poor church. Liberation theologian Jon Sobrino has written, ✱ "The poor keep alive the question of God, of his Kingdom, of Christ, of love, justice and sin" (Sobrino 1985, 97). The fact that worship takes place in communities of the urban poor is not a secret, of no relevance to the church outside those places. God's new order is celebrated and claimed among members of the same body who find themselves the under-valorized objects of global economic forces: the unemployed, underpaid, and those caught up in debt; migrants seeking security and work; refugees seeking safety and welcome.

> Genuine worship in a UPA [Urban Priority Area] church is of fundamental importance for those who live there and for the Church and society as a whole. . . . In the extreme situations of UPAs there is a sign of faith, hope and love that is desperately needed elsewhere too. (Ford and McFadyen 1995, 103–4)

While challenging the reshaping of the geography of power that we find in globalization and urbanization, Christians are called to live a real presence through transnational communities that include, strengthen, and give integrity to those at the margins. If we are to identify the neighbor we are called to love as anyone whom our activity or inactivity can affect, the task becomes truly global. Local pastoral praxis must then also be global political praxis. If the church can be truly present alongside the movements in the back alleys and with the poor on the fault lines of globalized society, catholic-ity reemerges as a vital trait of that presence, enacted and proclaimed most blatantly in the Eucharist. William Cava-naugh has described how the tension of global and local is to be found in the eucharistic act, which breaks down specific spatiality and unspecific universality, in favor of the catho-lic—"The *Catholica* is not a place . . . but a 'spatial story' about the origin and destiny of the whole world, a story en-acted in the Eucharist" (Cavanaugh 2000, 77).

Oikonomía—New Ordering?

A development of the themes of *koinonia* and God's new arrangements through the kingdom can be found in the fur-ther idea of the economy *(oikonomía)* of God. The origins of the concept lie in that of the household *(oikos),*[1] a system or unit in which people live, which is distinctive through its management or ordering. *Oikos* is the root for the economy and ecumenical—the ordering of life in a global dimension, persons and resources in relationship.

The economy that underpins God's new order is centered on "abundance and extraordinary generosity" epitomized in the gracious self-giving of God in Christ. David Ford con-siders this to be the ecclesiological challenge much urban theological practice lacks when it bases so much on a limited paternalistic understanding of the Pauline dictum "to re-member the poor."

> One question raised for contemporary ecclesiology by Paul's let-ters and their way of understanding all reality in terms of "the economy of God" is how comprehensive, Gospel-centred re-conception can be done today. [It] does help to enable an ethical and pragmatic consensus. But is this at the cost of not recognis-ing how deep the need is for the sort of redescription of reality, with the accompanying social expression that would enable some explicit thinking about the Church? (Ford 1989, 230)

In the teaching of Jesus, the economy of God is concerned with the reordering of relationships and resources through a just and gracious liberality. The parables indicate there is the possibility of imagining a different ordering; revalorization disrupts and overturns existing expectations. The sower reaps a harvest that will enable him to buy himself out of servitude (Mark 4:1–9). All the owners' energies are put into seeking the single lost coin or sheep until they are found (Luke 15:4–7, 8–10). The workers in the vineyard experience the economic implications of an order based on sufficiency and grace rather than obligation and honor[2] (Matt 20:1–16). Dives and Lazarus find their fortunes radically reversed (Luke 16:19–31).

For Paul, economy is the "Christ-centred activity of God" (Young and Ford 1988, 171). This is an economy of sufficiency and abundance, of mutuality and redistribution, which stands in sharp contrast with the scarcity-led, Rome-centered economy of the first-century Roman world that depended on a degrading system of relationships based on obligation and reciprocity. As God encourages generosity, the economy is about the possibility of new communities: a new pattern of relationship, internally and with other communities; it is an involving system that seeks to include and empower those who are not "economically active," which should not lack the gifts necessary to its life and mission. It is an economy with a critique that offers radical criteria for the valorization of people, places, and activities, concerned with bringing the experience of the future into the present in its exploration and embodiment of the possibilities that its experience of the Spirit makes possible.

The concern with the future and the ordering of God's *oikonomía* connects the church with a larger canvas. The household *(oikos)* in the broadest sense is not concerned just with the units in which people live, their societies and social order, but leads to fundamental ecological concerns. "Rooted in the household, its economic concern addresses the whole of the earth and all of creation—persons and resources in

their economic relationships—as a single, unified organism"
(Crosby 1988, 267).

*   Ecological concerns link Christians in with the bigger
story of creation and its liberation. These can never be considered a luxury but an essential aspect of the church's, and
particularly the urban church's, engagement with forces
that are antilife. As I have already stated, sustainability
thinking suggests ways in which communities need to review the impact they make through their internal life and
participation in wider networks. Sustainability integrates
concern with ecological resources with questions about
wholeness and integration, participation and responsibility,
social access and the quality of life. A church that is concerned about its own sustainability must have strategies
other than the growth paradigm, which openly assess its
impact and accountability in local and global terms. Sustainability thinking points us to the future; our action
or inaction now has consequences for communities and
congregations yet to come. Resilient communities are developed with a belief that future patterns of life can be
different if a distinct approach to change is initiated based
on a renewed theological understanding of justice, steward-
ship, and inclusion.

Notes

1. There is a need here to draw a distinction between this line of
thought and the later "patriarchalization" of the church apparent
in the household codes of Colossians, 1 Peter, and Ephesians (see
Schüssler Fiorenza 1983).

2. "While this parable primarily reveals a dimension of God's
reign, rather than strictly economic problems like (un)employment
and just wages, the experience of entering into God's house, into
God's economics (salvation), is predicated on human economics or
house reordering in the 'new age.' . . . By having the householder
pay the workers hired at the fifth hour the same as those who bore
the burden of the heat, Jesus shows that the ordering of the house
(i.e., economics) of God's reign involves certain characteristics: 1)
the land is God's; 2) God gives resources to every person who is

open; 3) God resources all people equally no matter how much or how hard they work; 4) the goal of resource-sharing is not 'more to those who do more' or 'less to those who do less,' but justice; 5) God's generosity *(hagathos)* stands opposed to the niggardliness *(poneros)* of humans; and 6) in contrast to that mentality that seems to legitimate 'more' for some, in God's reign there is enough for everyone" (Crosby 1988, 124).

Chapter Ten

Being Church—Engaging and Connecting

Place-Based Activities in the Space of Flows

What then does it mean in practice for the church to be present within and alongside the marginal communities that we are aware of in our global urban society? What praxis is appropriate in the layers of the global city? What are the challenges which our current praxis faces?

Robert Schreiter outlines a number of directions that are possible for practitioners of liberation theology in the new global context. He emphasizes the ambiguities of this context and the need for a flexibility in analysis and engagement. He explores the potential of a new social analysis that asks some fundamental questions of cherished ways of seeing things, as well as establishing the need for rethinking the location of evil—the demonization of globalization or informational capitalism are not credible options. In a networked world there is an indistinctiveness about "the old enemy," and new approaches will need to be developed to address the different layers and forms of global capitalism while exploiting its infrastructure. Schreiter cites the possibility suggested by some radical economists of the global South of creating new space as various capitalisms confront each other (Schreiter 1997, 106–7).

On the other hand, Schreiter acknowledges the possibility that "in the mode of a multipolar world, this is not the time for grand visions. One [could] concentrate instead upon building up the intermediate structures of society, strengthening neighbourhoods, urban zones, trade unions and political parties" (Schreiter 1997, 108). Schreiter prefers, however, the option of rethinking the agents of liberation theology and its tasks. The key tasks he identifies are *resistance*—maintaining and mobilizing struggles against tyranny; *denunciation*—assuming the prophetic role of identifying and condemning the source of evil and oppression, particularly in situations of denial; *critique*—uncovering and analyzing the ideological underpinning and connections inherent; *advocacy*—joining in solidarity in struggle, promoting specific projects, mobilizing people and resources; and *reconstruction*—identifying and acknowledging change and the possibility of moving into new situations through cooperation. I would want to suggest that the tasks Schreiter proposes are mediated in tensions and processes of those intermediate structures, making the urban environment the place where many of the contradictions of globalization need to be tackled. This will involve grappling with issues in the different strata of the global city. Our analysis, which Christian groups develop, must include what Castells describes as the development of "an awareness of the precise role of their place-based activities in the space of flows" (Castells 1989, 351).

The local presence of the church is in the midst of communities that are marginalized by the social forces we have been considering. To understand this better, I want to offer a few glimpses of how local-global challenges have changed the church and the praxis of those called to ministry, advocacy, prophecy, and engagement in the different strata, often on the fault lines, of the global city.

Docklands: Dispossession and the Recovery of Community

The first glimpse is a story from London, where transformation has taken place during the past eighteen years in an area of east London called the Isle of Dogs, part of what has become known as Docklands (see Foster 1999). The old dockyards closed in the early 1970s, leaving an area of high unemployment and multiple deprivation, alongside a wasteland of warehousing and deserted wharves. The area then became the subject of one of the largest development programs in Europe as the wharves were turned over to a project to accommodate the exploding financial services sector in new state-of-the-art office blocks alongside expensive riverside apartments. It was a textbook example of how globalization creates significant sites where certain activities, the places in which they happen, the people who perform those activities, and the places in which they live become sharply overvalorized, in comparison with other places, activities, and people.

Local residents saw the wasteland transformed by the government-created London Docklands Development Corporation (LDDC), an autonomous body with no local accountability. The initial development provided few new job opportunities, and eight thousand people found themselves literally living on a building site, with neglected public services, alienated and angry, with little opportunity to strike back. About the same time, members of the Bangladeshi community, already a significant presence in east London, began to move into the area. This in many ways reflected the global trends described by Michael Safier:

> Recent trends in cities throughout the world . . . have made clear the realities—and the prospects—of increasingly uncertain, generally unsatisfactory and dangerously unequal ways of living. . . . An accelerated trend towards "private affluence and public squalor" has been accompanied by a decline in the standards of both amenity and civility, with a "transnational" elite and a "marginal" underclass competing for available space. (Safier 1993, 34)

A previously working-class community felt it was being colonized. The lightning conductor that attracted this resentment in the end was not the developers but the Bangladeshi community, which became the victim of mindless acts of racism and public gossip. They were accused of jumping the housing waiting list and having preferential treatment through welfare services. Much of this activity was orchestrated or encouraged by the British National Party, a fascist organization that often targets areas of unease and social transition. In 1993, in a local government by-election on the Isle of Dogs, a member of the BNP was elected as a councilor for the Millwall Ward, a division of the London borough of Tower Hamlets. This election sent shockwaves through east London and the rest of the country, as the first election of an openly fascist politician since the 1930s.

In the confusion and fragmentation that followed, the local church leaders began to respond by sensitively, piece by piece, offering an alternative hope for that community through speaking the truth about what was happening. Their strategy was to build bridges between the local white and Bangladeshi populations; to challenge the developers regarding the impact of their reshaping of the area; and strengthen the electoral process in the run-up to the next election. The LDDC and developers soon found that this local contestation of space and identity had implications for business; companies did not want to relocate to an area associated with extreme politics and were anxious to look at ways of improving community relations. Drawing in neighborhood projects, the mainline political parties, and minority ethnic groups, the church leaders' strategy built on community organizing, raising awareness through work in schools, and a careful handling of the outside media, which wished to sensationalize the situation. This also involved confronting racism in the body of Christ as well as the injustice created in that community. Under the slogan "Celebrate the Difference" a "Rainbow Ribbon Campaign" was initiated by the churches—eventually using over a mile of ribbon cut into short lengths. Win or lose, there was a determination to create a new awareness of the shared responsibility for the future of that community, which rejected the BNP in the next election (see Holtam and Mayo 1998; Carnelley 1998).

The churches stood by the local population through the changes, while developing a prophetic praxis that goes beyond self-interest and advocates those who have no voice at the location of power. Urban regeneration schemes are often not the good news for the poor they claim to be but are rather orientated to the needs of local governments and developers. The movement on the Isle of Dogs created a "local culture of urgency" (Castells 1997, 64) that challenged the assumptions about the place and its community—was Docklands a wasteland waiting for development or home to a significant number of people who had a personal stake in its future?

The church must stand with urban communities in the midst of the shakings of globalization; this will involve living alongside the anger, the pain, and the misunderstanding of those areas, and the churches may need to be prepared to take the brunt of it. The initiative emphasized the determination of Christians to stay part of a community that found itself fragmented and dispossessed. In the global context, it is on such fault lines that the church needs to locate itself. "The triumph of the churches on the Isle of Dogs is that they did not sleep through it all as many do" (Holtam and Mayo 1998, 21).

Making Connections

The next glimpse concerns how Christian pressure groups can begin to engage with these issues and develop new patterns of work. Church Action on Poverty has campaigned for nearly twenty years on issues of poverty in the UK, with an emphasis on increasing awareness of domestic poverty through enabling the voice of those experiencing poverty to be heard in national forums. Christian Aid is the leading ecumenical relief and development agency for the British churches, concerned primarily with poverty in the global South and a key driving force behind Jubilee 2000. These two agencies came together through an increasing awareness of the global impact of economic change and the need to share wider strategies to tackle poverty. A number of programs have been identified, through which the concerns of those experiencing poverty and addressing these issues in global North and global South can be brought together. The three key elements of the project were a North-South community exchange program (linking a partner agency, SamaSama, in Manila, and a Church Action on Poverty group from Thornaby-on-Tees in northeast England); consultations on globalization, poverty, and local economic initiatives; and the publication of reports on the lessons being learned.

The exchange visits deliberately involve those who live with poverty, particularly those involved in self-help and community development programs, not just those who work with and for them through nongovernmental organizations. The visits were not intended as exposure but part of an ongoing program to identify strategies and mutuality in the struggle for human dignity. The groups have found connections between their contexts—merchant seamen from northeast England have been replaced by Filipino sailors; transnational companies have operated factories in both areas; common practices of exploitation, including low wages and homeworking and the ubiquitous presence of loan sharks. They also discovered shared strategies for creating alternative resources and developing community capacity—particularly credit unions and the opening of microcredit facilities; in addition, the British group hopes to learn from SamaSama's community education work. Sharing differences has also been important—not least the different forms that poverty takes, and how it is compounded by other aspects of social exclusion. The Filipino group found poverty in the global North, where they did not believe it existed; the British group have found themselves involved in advocacy work regarding issues of aid and development.

The consultations have formed the program for Church Action on Poverty's National Poverty Consultations in 1997 and 2001. These have been aimed particularly at those promoting greater economic literacy through Christian agencies, fair trade work, and local initiatives. An initial report, *Local Lives and Livelihoods in a Global Economy,* was published in November 1999 (Bundell 1999). The report acknowledged the continuing presence of the churches in poor communities and the need to "bring moral arguments to the globalisation, exclusion and poverty debates."

The collaboration between Christian Aid and Church Action on Poverty is a significant example of how agencies and networks that have pursued different agendas find themselves connected in the world of global capitalism. The local groups involved in the exchange have come to appreciate the enormity of the forces shaping the world—not least, how global, capital-based organizations "select their locations at their convenience, playing localized social and political actors one against the other" (Castells 1989, 352). Through the exchange groups, concerned very definitely with communities of place, have developed that "awareness of the precise role of their place-based activities in the space of flows" (Castells 1989, 351) and have been renewed in their determination to be part of the struggle and imagination for a just future for all.

Los Angeles: Organizing and Resistance

Within this new global economic formation the local struggle takes on a new significance. The human dimension of restructuring asserts itself through struggles for justice, through the networking and the awareness that can be raised, as local questions are posed to corporations or at the cores of the strategic global sites. Saskia Sassen could be writing of Docklands, Manila, Los Angeles, or Mexico City:

> The uncomfortable question is whether the sudden growth in homelessness . . . the growth of poverty generally, the growth of low-wage employment without any fringe benefits, and the growth of sweatshops and industrial homework are all linked to the growth of an industrial complex orientated to the world market and significantly less dependent on local factors. . . . To this should be added the growth of what amounts to an ideology of globalism, whereby localities are seen as powerless in an era of global economic forces. (Sassen 2001, 340)

New patterns of resistance and advocacy by local alliances, which include but are not exclusively church groups, take on new significance, and this is particularly apparent in campaigns directed at the conditions of low-wage labor. These campaigns are developing the social and economic literacy I have already described and relating it to conditions of employment in local situations in Europe and North America, but also connecting their analysis to global conditions. Campaigns for a "living wage" (regional variations often mean that a nationally set "minimum wage" is inadequate in economic "hotspots") seek to address the needs of low-skilled workers, who find themselves taking on extra hours or additional jobs in their struggle to maintain shelter, food, and family in the face of a soaring cost of living.

Valle and Torres have written that "it is already clear the global city's culture-based and information-based mode of production is premised on a surplus of low paid, mostly immigrant labor" (Valle and Torres 2000, 104); this is nowhere more apparent than in Los Angeles, where a considerable shift has taken place in the work force. With migration from Mexico and the Asian Pacific Rim, by 1990 Latinos accounted for over 50 percent of workers in manufacturing and service industries in Los Angeles county. Levels of labor organization have fallen with the disappearance of large-scale, labor-intensive, "fordist," styles of manufacturing in which unions were strong. The mostly immigrant work force in the public sector, as well as the new service and low-skilled manufacturing industries, have been low-paid, temporary, and initially unorganized. Rebuilding labor organization in Los Angeles has been a long-term struggle involving changing the culture and methods of the unions—the necessity of a bilingual operation has accompanied the transformation of unions into "social movements." Old methods would not work; striking workers in the hotel sector could be easily sacked and the latest arrivals hired. The new movement saw its strength in its ability to organize members and allies for new strategies, often drawing on the skills learned in Mexican and Latin American labor struggles, as well as their ability to exploit the "media-saturated environment" in which they worked (Valle and

Torres 2000, 106). The local political struggles of Los Angeles, a key site in global culture and economy, are a crucial example of how the contradictions and forms of globalization collide and play at many levels. This is what Sassen refers to as "a new politics of traditionally disadvantaged actors operating in this new transnational economic geography" (Sassen 2000, 49). And it is into that new politics that church people are finding themselves increasingly drawn.

Richard Gillett describes the involvement of a group of faith leaders (Clergy and Laity United for Economic Justice-CLUE) in the campaign to enact a "living wage ordinance" in Los Angeles (Gillett 2002), with a particular emphasis on workers in the hotel sector and companies with contracts from the city authorities. CLUE members were able to participate in "actions" alongside union and community campaigners, as well as later initiate their own strategy of letter writing, direct action ("sit-in, preach-in" tactics in hotel restaurants), and an interfaith procession drawing on the images of Holy Week and Passover as bitter herbs or milk and honey were offered to hotel management—raising both public awareness and targeting hotels which had not complied with demands for justice. Gillett describes how the campaign brought clergy and laity into contact not just with the underside of the glittering prosperity of California, but with the people who make up the new waves of cross-border migration in the globalized economy. Many of the union organizers "were Latino, like many of the workers themselves; several key union leaders in the city are themselves former farm workers" (Gillett 2002, 35). Such encounters were vital in understanding the complexities of the human change that globalization is bringing about.

> The reality that increasingly assaults workers not only in Los Angeles but across the globe is that what belongs to them as workers, namely their dignity and respect and their right to a living wage has been taken away from them. (Gillett 2002, 37)

Gillett describes the essential task to identify "handles [a concrete and visible challenge] to address the economic injustices of a corporate capitalism that appears to sublimate even national sovereignty and cultural particularities to the inevitability of the 'bottom line' " (Gillett 2002, 38).

It is not just local labor issues that the church people have taken on in the global economy. Congregational organizing has been effective in holding corporations to account for working conditions in clothing sweatshops in central America and Asia, as well as closer to home (See Dyson 1999).

Naming the Challenges

The situations described offer glimpses of the challenges facing Christian groups that engage with the forces perceived in the local context behind which lie global forces and flows. When we set up a local drugs project, do we think for one moment of the global systems that are needed to get those drugs from the coca fields of Latin America to the streets of, say, Chicago? What are the global forces at work that create the pockets of employment that our training projects seek to address? These engagements will not necessarily be perceived as global battles: more often they are street-level ministries to the dispossessed in the urban context. In a globalizing world we become increasingly aware of shared urban realities: street children, HIV, housing, exclusion poverty and powerlessness, racism/minorities, drugs, the gun culture, and microviolence. Behind many of these statistics with human faces can lie sophisticated clandestine organizations, many of which cross frontiers with the same ease as globalized capital. Writing in *Sojourners,* Bill Wylie Kellerman paints a terrifying profile of the drugs trade as a global and a spiritual power:

> To comprehend drugs as a power means, at a minimum, to see it whole, as an entity, a configuration of competing underground corporations, economic arrangements, illegitimate operations, and cultural forms. It means seeing the complex system of transnational–national enterprises as an economic entity that reaches across the planet. Between the poppy or coca fields and the hustling street vendor lies this huge enterprise. In certain

respects it is a network marketing operation (of the variety mastered legally by Amway) with a 700 to 2,000 per cent mark-up from one end to the other. Moreover, it conforms to the patterns of two-tiered global economy. Above élites dominate production, manufacture and global export; with a middle management operation over-seeing regional distribution, paramilitary security, money laundering and the like. Below are the peasant farmers and the crackhouses or their equivalent feeding on cheap labour. Once again, at both ends the same weapons, the same methods of enforcement, the same violence proliferates. (Wylie Kellerman 1996)

Similar portraits might be written of the trafficking of asylum seekers, the trade in small arms, and the abuse of children through underage labor, pedophile rings, or their covert movement.

If we take seriously our dialogue with others concerned with the issues that confront us about the new forces shaping our urban areas, I believe we will find a possibility for a truly negotiated settlement, which draws on the human resources—experience, hopes, aspirations, energy—that is located in the life of urban communities. Beyond the physical environment we must be aware that local urban change is interconnected by the social, technological, and economic changes that are global processes. As we address the realities of the local context we must not be afraid to speak of their connectivity with complex issues and systems as we find ourselves in new, often bewildering territory. Christian presence in the urban world needs to speak the truth of what is happening as it struggles to create communities and networks that are active in the laying of new foundations as part of the healing, redeeming, and transformation of those cities. From an African context, Aylward Shorter writes:

> The Christian task in Africa is the evangelization of a continent in the process of rapid urbanization. In fact, it is, to a great extent, the evangelization of the urbanization process itself. If the Gospel of Christ makes a lasting impact in Africa, it will be because it has helped the urban process to become less invidious and less unjust, more human, more enduringly creative. It will have given the African town a soul. (Shorter 1991, 148)

What might this mean on other continents or in a global context? Do Christians have the audacity to believe that they can evangelize the global processes through their local and transnational witness? Alongside other movements, churches ✳ can encourage practices of resistance and critique—developing the capacity and vision of communities to organize themselves and plan for a different future. The churches may find that it is their existing transnational character that enables these practices to be disseminated and connected on a global basis. To engage with and shape our urban future(s), it is our responsibility as Christian disciples to be developing models of urban theological practice that are aware and adequate for the task to which we are called. There is a need to rediscover the spirituality of place in the potential of urban life, through its vibrancy, diversity, and conviviality, as well the possibility of interaction and change. Those engaged in urban theology must be active new communities built on the visions and imagination of ordinary urban people, as part of the healing, redeeming, and transformation of our neighborhoods and cities, and our urbanizing, globalizing world.

Chapter Eleven

Faith in the Future of an Urbanizing World

Contesting the Urban Future

As we have seen, much is being written on the future of our urban society. Urbanologists, sociologists, economists, geographers, as well as governments, nongovernmental oranizations, and corporate interests all strive to get a handle on the form of that future in a global perspective. The commentators we have encountered, such as the Urban 21 Commission and Leonie Sandercock, look for ways that the trends might be realigned through government intervention or insurgent planning practice; Manuel Castells looks for potential to initiate bottom-up change through citizens or social movements. The determination that the future can be different—must be different—underlies secular and religious thinking about the cities that our urban communities will become.

The ability to draw on imagination, observation, and experience opens the possibility of engaging with that future. A "utopian vision," writes Castells, "is needed to shake the institution from short-sightedness and stasis to enable people to think the unthinkable, thus enhancing their awareness and control of the inevitable social transformation" (Castells 1989, 353). These futures that are imagined can be dystopian as well as utopian; they may draw on the experience of the past as well as the lure of the future, but their power lies in their ability to challenge the present.

> When looking at future scenarios for Los Angeles—probably the most written-about urban conglomeration of our time—Mike Davis writes of *"excavating the future."* Davis recognizes that the concerns about the future in one particular location in our rapidly urbanizing and globalizing world draw deeply

on experience and experiments with other possible futures, whether it is the transient dreams of Hollywood, the optimism of the socialist collectives of the frontier; the actualization of the *Bladerunner* nightmare in the downtown architecture of incarceration;[1] or the LA School's "postmodern mapping" of the present as they reconstruct the sociological and geographical narrative and rhetoric. For this latter group "the city is a place where everything is possible, nothing is safe and durable enough to believe in, where constant synchronicity prevails, and the automatic ingenuity of capital ceaselessly throws up new forms and spectacles." (Davis 1992, 86)

Cyberpunk writer William Gibson is the novelist most closely associated with Davis's vision. Gibson's ability to give terminology and conceptuality to an emergent world of technology and spatial intensity is accompanied by a vision that goes beyond the benign technological visions of politicians to the reality of the people who will be the "underclass" of the new order. Gibson's second trilogy (1994; 1996; 1999) depicts such a society in a postearthquake California. The middle class has disappeared, leaving a postcapitalist élite who control and party, ever on the move across a world where one office and reception look much like another; and an urban underclass that exists in autonomous zones (a shanty town on a crumbling bridge or a holiday complex on a contaminated beach) from which they enter the technopoles as scavengers. Globalization has reached its hiatus as supermarkets, music, and food become indistinguishable on either side of the Pacific; corporate power is an unseen actor, often demanding sacrifice and retribution.

In many ways this trilogy, and its predecessor which began with mold-breaker *Neuromancer* (Gibson 1984), is a new apocalyptic unveiling, a prefigurative sociology that lies close to the surface of our experience of the present, not least our inabilities to come to comprehend the full potential of the technologies and social processes we already find around us. As corporations struggle to control the consequences of technological development, they find that the imagination they have unleashed cannot be contained through scientific patents or property rights. Gibson's heroes (in a very classical sense of that word) struggle for space and salvation against commercial and cultural powers that undermine the imagination and human integrity. That space may be found in the nether regions of cyberspace or the alternative economy of the bridge. The world that they inhabit groans with innovation: as computer systems become more and more complex, dissidents reactivate the hardware of the late twentieth century to understand the computer architecture upon which all subsequent technology has been based. It is a world where excessive detail has excluded the imagination and the spontaneous, where the resources to allow possibility need to be fought for.

A Taoist hit man, the owner of a simple but effective ceramic knife, compares it with the other weapons of the street: "That which is overdesigned, too highly specific, anticipates outcome; the anticipation of outcome guarantees, if not failure, the absence of grace" (Gibson 1999, 133). (It may be in other instruments and forms that we need to struggle for grace in the urban future.)

David Harvey ends his recent book, _Spaces of Hope,_ with a dream of an urban society that is communitarian and strives for human and ecological balance, made possible only through environmental disaster and economic meltdown. He recalls the questioning of philosopher Ernst Bloch, who wondered why it was that "possibility has had such a bad press?" (Harvey 2000, 258). Harvey's utopia probes notions of freedom and privacy, of hierarchy and network, of mutuality and obligation; while not a blueprint, it brings into contrast the present and the near future, insisting "that things could and must be better":

> If, as most of us believe, we have the power to shape the world according to our visions and desires then how come we have collectively made such a mess of it? Our social and physical world can and must be made, remade, and if that goes awry, remade yet again. Where to begin and what is to be done are the key questions. (Harvey 2000, 281)

Space, Place, and Grace—Believing in the Future

Our common future is too important to leave in the hands of ✳
politicians, economists, and global business executives. With
neighbors, we need to reassert the need for the urban future
to be a social, not individual, project. This will involve investment in the signs of hope we find in the present—hints of
confidence built in disempowered communities; of glimpses
of new bridges, connections, and networks being built between people—enabling solidarity; of pre-echoes of change,
as awkward questions are asked of the assumptions of the
present. As Sandercock says of the examples she uses, "these
values are already active, and actively contested . . . [w]e can
learn from them what is and is not *Cosmopolis*, and how to
make these practices flourish" (Sandercock 1998, 200).

The events which were witnessed in New York and Washington on 11 September 2001 were not *Cosmopolis*. The pictures which were flashed on television screens and Internet
news sites, so quickly, looked like scenes from the most har-
rowing films where the unreal rips into the everyday life of
the city causing carnage and chaos. The symbolism of the
attacks on the World Trade Center is significant to many of
the concerns of this book. The buildings have been described
as both "the most monumental figure of Western urban development" (de Certeau 1984, 93) and "a monument of
global capitalism" (Mendieta 2001, 399).

> A city is the epicentre of the encounter of several vectors of
> force. Cities are always about people, first and foremost. Before
> cities are structures of stone and steel, cement, glass and fibre
> optics they are about the concentration of human activity,
> labour, power, initiative of human beings. . . . The skyline of a
> city and its physiognomy is always the result of that encounter.
> (Mendieta 2001, 399)

The global aftermath of the attacks has raised questions
about the *cosmopolitan* nature of our cities, concerns of
urban security, the desirability of tall "trophy" buildings,
and the perceptions (if not realities) of the globalization

project. There is a vulnerability in urban living which city leaders and planners rarely acknowledge, though one which others cities have experienced, such as London during the bombing campaigns of the IRA.

Archbishop Rowan Williams, who was in the vicinity of Wall Street at the time of the attacks, perceives wider issues of vulnerability and security in the connections between the life of the city and its economic divisions:

> The horror of being vulnerable to terrorist violence might open our eyes to the vulnerability that in fact underlies the whole globalization process. It is harder to believe that our world is one in which the increase of wealth for a minority can be indefinitely projected without cost. Already the existence of wealthy residential developments surrounded by all the technological refinements of security in many of our cities tells us that the spiral of wealth is also the spiral of threat. (Williams 2002, 61)

The events of 11 September while unique in their strategy and exposure were not unprecedented attacks on the life and dynamism of urban community. Michael Safier puts the attacks in the context of at least twenty other acts of *urbicide*—"the deliberate destruction and/or disintegration of an entire way of living in a city, by means of both killing its citizens and maiming its culture of civility and diversity" (Safier 2001, 416). Sarajevo, Belfast, Oklahoma City, Banja Luka, Jerusalem, Kabul, Mogadishu, Baghdad all tells stories of such attacks—some limited and partial, others devastating, involving tens of thousands of people and the "negation of all normal urban existence, both literal—in physical terms—and even more significantly symbolic—in terms of such values as liberty, civility, diversity and co-existence" (Safier 2001, 422) by civil conflict, terrorism, and international action. Traditions of and reputations for coexistence, cultural pluralism, and openness are easily destroyed and impossible to rebuild after genocide or the uprooting of people. These dangers are inherent in the responses to 11 September in many cities where fear of otherness became apparent in attacks on Middle Eastern and Asian immigrant communities, as the fundamentalisms of the global stage became apparent in local arenas. The initiatives into which Christians and people of other faiths were drawn emphasized the need for a revitalized understanding and celebration of human community lived in diversity and open with an explicit propensity to include and absorb newcomers of many kinds. In many places this has allowed the emergence of new alliances and new patterns of civic leadership. Such determination was well expressed by Peter Marcuse:

> Make it clear the city is a welcoming city for all peoples, that we do not confuse culture with cause, that we are and will remain an international city and a multicultural city; brag about it. (Marcuse 2001, 397)

We cannot tell which specific elements of symbolism were in the minds of the attackers on 11 September. For the majority of people the world was not changed; the global trends and processes described in this book continue unabated in our urban areas. The city proved vulnerable; it can be shaken; yet the lives of its poor carry on. Racism, fundamentalism, islamophobia all attempt to spread rumors of those who are other and the threat they pose. Any response must be lived through whatever cultural, political, communal, legal, and social means that are available. A leading Asian-British novelist wrote of the urgency thus: "If both racism and fundamentalism are diminishers of life—reducing others to extractions—the effort of culture must be to keep others alive by describing and celebrating their intricacy, by seeing that this is not only of value but a necessity" (Hanif Kureishi, *The Guardian,* 5 April 2002).

Christians are called to participate in these efforts as active citizens, storytellers, and prophets. Walter Wink has suggested that "history belongs to the intercessors who believe the future into being" (Wink 1998, 187). I have already noted the power of worship to lift and sacralize the reality of place through the celebration and claims of God's new order—*on earth as it is in heaven.* Imagination is part of the potential that must be released if that future is to be claimed, *believed in:* an imagination that refuses to accept the daily visions on our television screens of *hell on earth,* that can harness the energy in the alliances that are forged, the networks that are consolidated, and the physical spaces that are actualized. It will be our urban places in which this realignment must take place. It may be less a case of resisting the science-fiction future of the movies but rather of resisting the ways in which our urban places are molded into the great plans of corporate expansion and cultural industries; of challenging the assumptions made when places and their communities are demonized for political ends; of opposing places designed to exclude or dehumanize; of refusing to accept the valorization of places in schemes that colonize areas and price people out of their homes; of offering "global hospitality" in the presence of death (Williams 2002, 64). Peter Marcuse imagines the concrete nature of place: "We need cities that will be conditions of life, of full and free unfragmented lives, not cities of discretion and domination; we need walls that welcome and shelter, not walls that exclude and oppress" (Marcuse 1994, 251).

*   To be realistic is to acknowledge the flexibility that will be needed in an urbanizing, globalizing world; the prescriptive, single course of action is not the task, nor is the nostalgic dependence on neatly structured models of organization. In the midst of this process we are called to create a culture of urgency, to identify a moment of *kairos*[2] that offers opportunity as well as possibility, a *kairos* which grasped and lived overtakes the moment of *crisis.* Castells writes about the "reconstruction of meaning in the space of flows" and the need to read the signs of resistance. "Societies are not made up of passive subjects resigned to structural domination. The meaninglessness of places, the powerlessness of political institutions are resented and resisted, individually and collectively by a variety of social actors" (Castells 1989, 350).

*   We need to be aware of the subtlety of the plot as well as its more obvious intrusions into all aspects of life. It is in urban places, on the fault lines and in the back alleys of our global society, that the vision and priority for our faith communities must be to allow room for grace to flourish in the reshaping of our space, our relationships, and our environment for justice, infusing them with the imagination of hope.

Notes

1. The cover of the paperback edition of Davis's book carries a photo of the Metropolitan Detention Center in downtown Los Angeles—a futuristic building with more in common with the architecture of hotels or convention centers, "a 'distinguished' addition to Downtown's continuum of security and design." An inmate whispers to Davis during his tour of the installation: "Can you imagine the mind**** of being locked up in a Holiday Inn?" (Davis 1992, 257).

2. That is a decisive point in time—of judgment and the breaking in of God's new order (Mark 1:15; Rom 13:11).

References and Further Reading

Chapter 1: Encountering the Urban

References

Borden, Iain, et al., eds. 2001. *The Unknown City: Contesting Architecture and Social Space.* Cambridge, Mass.: MIT Press.

Clark, David. 1996. *Urban World/Global City.* London and New York: Routledge.

De Gruchy, John. 1987. *Theology and Ministry in Context and Crisis: A South African Approach.* London: Collins Flame.

Eastman, Theodore. 1986. "Mission of Christ in Urban America." *Crossroads Are for Meeting.* Edited by Philip Turner and Frank Sugeno. Sewanee, Tenn.: SPCK USA.

Greenhalgh, Liz, and Ken Worpole. 1997. "The Convivial City." *Life after Politics: New Thinking for the Twenty-First Century.* Edited by Geoff Mulgan. London: Fontana.

Inwood, Stephen. 1998. *A History of London.* London: Macmillan; New York: Carroll & Graf.

Leech, Kenneth. 2001. *Through Our Long Exile.* London: Darton, Longman & Todd.

Marx, Karl. 1976. *Collected Works.* Vol. 5. Moscow: Progress Publishers.

Massey, Doreen, John Allen, and Steve Pile. 1999. *City Worlds.* London and New York: Routledge.

Sandercock, Leonie. 1998. *Towards Cosmopolis—Planning for Multicultural Cities.* Chichester and New York: John Wiley & Sons.

Schreiter, Robert. 1997. *The New Catholicity: Theology between the Global and the Local.* Maryknoll, N.Y.: Orbis.

Sheldrake, Philip. 2000. *Spaces for the Sacred: Place, Memory, Identity.* London: SCM Press.

United Nations. 1996. *An Urbanizing World: Global Report on Human Settlements 1996.* Oxford: Oxford University Press.

Further Reading

Allen, John, Doreen Massey, and Michael Pryke. 1999. *Unsettling Cities: Movement/Settlement.* London and New York: Routledge.

Eade, John, ed. 1997. *Living the Global City—Globalization as Local Process.* London and New York: Routledge.

Hall, Tim. 2000. *Urban Geography.* London and New York: Routledge.

Northcott, Michael, ed. 1998. *Urban Theology: A Reader.* London and Herndon Va.: Cassell.

Pile, Steve, Christopher Brook, and Gerry Mooney. 1999. *Unruly Cities? Order/Disorder.* London and New York: Routledge.

Journals

CITY—Analysis of Urban Trends, Culture Theory, Policy, Action. Carfax Publishing Ltd, Taylor and Francis Ltd, Rankine Road, Basingstoke, Hants, RG24 8PR; 325 Chestnut Street, 8th Floor, Philadelphia, PA 19106. Online: www.tandf.co.uk/journals/carfax/13604813.html.

Environment & Urbanization. IIED, 3 Endsleigh Street, London WC1H 0DD. Online: www.iied.org.

Global Outlook. International Urban Research Monitor. Woodrow Wilson International Center for Scholars, 1 Woodrow Wilson Plaza, 1300 Pennsylvania Avenue, Washington, DC 20004. Online: www.huduser.org/publications/urbaff/goutlook.html.

Chapter 2: Being Urban, Being Global

References

Buffoni, Laura. 1997. "Rethinking Poverty in Globalized Conditions." *Living the Global City—Globalization as Local Process.* Edited by John Eade. London and New York: Routledge.

Chung, Chuihua Judy, Jeffrey Inaba, Rem Koolhaas, Sze Tsung Leong, eds. 2001. *Harvard Design School: Guide to Shopping.* Cambridge, Mass.: Harvard Design School.

Clark, David. 1996. *Urban World/Global City.* London and New York: Routledge.

Cochrane, Allan. 2000. "The Social Construction of Urban Policy." *A Companion to the City.* Edited by Gary Bridges and Sophie Watson. Oxford and Malden, Mass.: Blackwell.

Davey, Andrew. 1999. "Globalization as Challenge and Opportunity in Urban Mission: An Outlook from London." *International Review of Mission* (October): 381–89.

Department for Environment Transport and the Regions. 2000. *Urban White Paper: Our Towns and Cities: The Future. Delivering an Urban Renaissance.* London: The Stationery Office. Online: www.urban.odpm.gov.uk/whitepaper/ourtowns/index.htm.

Duany, Andres, Elizabeth Plater-Zyberk, and Jeff Speck. 2000. *Suburban Nation: The Rise of Sprawl and the Decline of the American Dream.* New York: North Point Press.

Faramelli, Norman, Edward Rodman, and Anne Scheibner. 1996. "Seeking to Hear and to Heed in the Cities: Urban Ministry in the Postwar Episcopal Church." *Churches, Cities, and Human Community: Urban Ministry in the United States 1945–1985.* Edited by Clifford J. Green. Grand Rapids, Mich.: Eerdmans.

Giddens, Anthony. 1994. *Beyond Left and Right.* Cambridge: Polity Press; Stanford, Calif.: Stanford University Press.

Girardet, Herbert. 2000. "Greening Urban Society." *Ethics and the Built Environment*. Edited by Warwick Fox. London and New York: Routledge.

Gray, John. 1999. *False Dawn: The Delusions of Global Capitalism*. London: Granta Books; New York: The New Press.

Harvey, David. 1996. *Justice, Nature, and the Geographies of Difference*. Oxford and Malden, Mass.: Blackwell.

Massey, Doreen. 1994. *Space, Place, and Gender*. Cambridge: Polity Press; Minneapolis: University of Minnesota Press.

Orsi, Robert, ed. 1999. *Gods of the City: Religions and the American Urban Landscape*. Bloomington and Indianapolis: Indiana University Press.

Pahl, R. E. 1970. *Patterns of Urban Life*. London: Longman.

Robertson, Roland. 1992. *Globalization: Social Theory and Global Culture*. London and Thousand Oaks, Calif.: Sage.

Rogers, Richard. 1999. *Towards an Urban Renaissance— Final Report of the Urban Task Force, chaired by Lord Rogers of Riverside*. London: E&FN Spon.

Safier, Michael. 1996. "The Cosmopolitan Challenge in Cities on the Edge of the Millennium: Moving from Conflict to Coexistence." *CITY—Analysis of Urban Trends, Culture, Theory, Policy, Action*, 3–4 (June): 12–29.

Satterthwaite, David, ed. 1999. *The Earthscan Reader in Sustainable Cities*. London and Sterling, Va.: Earthscan Publications.

Sennett, Richard. 2000. "The Art of Making Cities." London School of Economics Public Lecture, 9 March, reprinted in *New Statesman*, 5 June, 25–27.

Thompson, Grahame. 2000. "Economic Globalization?" *A Globalizing World? Culture, Economics, Politics*. Edited by David Held. London and New York: Routledge.

Wackernagel, Mathis, and William Rees. 1996. *Our Ecological Footprint: Reducing Human Impact on the Earth*. Gabiola Island, B.C.: New Society Publishers.

Further Reading

Abraham, K. C. 1996. "Globalization: A Gospel and Culture Perspective." *International Review of Mission*, 85–92.

Amin, Ash, and Nigel Thrift. 2002. *Cities: Reimagining the Urban*. Cambridge: Polity Press.

Eade, John, and Christopher Mele. 2002. *Understanding the City: Contemporary and Future Perspectives*. Oxford and Malden, Mass.: Blackwell.

Fainstein, Susan, and Scott Campbell, eds. 1996. *Readings in Urban Theory*. Oxford and Malden, Mass.: Blackwell.

Giddens, Anthony. 2000. *Runaway World: How Globalization Is Reshaping Our Lives*. London: Profile Books; New York: Routledge.

Held, David, Anthony McGrew, David Goldblatt, and Jonathan Perraton. 1999. *Global Transformations: Politics, Economics, and Culture*. Cambridge: Polity Press; Stanford, Calif.: Stanford University Press.

Lechner, Frank J., and John Boli. 2000. *The Globalization Reader*. Oxford and Malden, Mass.: Blackwell.

Potter, Robert, and Sally Lloyd Evans. 1998. *The City in the Developing World*. London: Longman.

Rogers, Richard. 1997. *Cities for a Small Planet*. London: Faber; Boulder, Colo.: Westview Press.

Waters, Malcolm. 1995. *Globalization*. London and New York: Routledge.

Weyland, Petra, and Ayse Once, eds. 1998. *Space, Culture, and Power—New Identities in Globalizing Cities*. London and Atlantic Highlands, N.J.: Zed Books.

Chapter 3: Urban Sites and Global Places

References

Atherton, John. 2000. *Public Theology for Changing Times*. London: SPCK.

Castells, Manuel. 1997. *The Power of Identity*. Vol. 2 of *The Information Age: Economy, Society, and Culture*. Oxford and Malden, Mass.: Blackwell.

————. 2000a. *The Rise of the Network Society*. Vol. 1 of *The Information Age: Economy, Society, and Culture*. 2d ed. Oxford and Malden, Mass.: Blackwell.

————. 2000b. *The End of Millennium*. Vol. 3 of *The Information Age: Economy, Society, and Culture*. 2d ed. Oxford and Malden, Mass.: Blackwell.

Castells, Manuel, and Peter Hall. 1994. *Technopoles of the World: The Making of Twenty-First Century Industrial Complexes*. London and New York: Routledge.

Cox, Harvey. 1996. *Fire from Heaven: The Rise of Pentecostal Spirituality and the Reshaping of Religion in the Twenty-First Century*. London: Cassell; New York: Perseus Books.

Davey, Andrew. 1998. "London as Theological Problem." *Theology* (May CI/801): 188–96.

Dempster, Murray W., Byron D. Klaus, and Douglas Petersen, eds. 1999. *The Globalization of Pentecostalism: A Religion Made to Travel*. Oxford and Irvine, Calif.: Regnum Books International.

Green, Laurie. 2000. *The Impact of the Global: An Urban Theology*. Sheffield: Urban Theology Unit.

Gunnell, Barbara, and David Timms, eds. 2000. *After Seattle: Globalization and Its Discontents*. London: Catalyst.

Harvey, David. 2000. "Cosmopolitanism and the Banality of Geographical Evils." *Popular Culture: Society for Transnational Cultural Studies* 12, no. 2 (spring): 529–64.

Magnusson, Walter. 2000. "Politicizing the Global City." *Democracy, Citizenship, and the Global City*. Edited by Engin F. Isin. London and New York: Routledge.

Massey, Doreen. 1994. *Space, Place, and Gender*. Cambridge: Polity Press; Minneapolis: University of Minnesota Press.

Ottley, James. 2000. "The Debt Crisis in Theological Perspective." *The Local Church in a Global Age: Reflections for a New Century*. Edited by Max Stackhouse, Tim Dearborn, and Scott Paeth. Grand Rapids, Mich.: Eerdmans.

Sandercock, Leonie. 1998. *Towards Cosmopolis—Planning for Multicultural Cities*. Chichester and New York: John Wiley & Sons.

Sassen, Saskia. 1998. *Globalization and Its Discontents.* New York: The New Press.

———. 2000a. *Cities in a Global Economy.* 2d ed. London and Thousand Oaks, Calif.: Pine Forge Press.

———. 2000b. "The Global City: Strategic Site/New Frontier." *Democracy, Citizenship, and the Global City.* Edited by Engin F. Isin. London and New York: Routledge.

Zincone, Giovanna, and John Agnew. 2000. "The Second Great Transformation: The Politics of Globalisation in the Global North." *Space & Polity* 4, no. 1 (May 2000): 5–21.

Further Reading

Castells. Manuel. 1989. *The Informational City: Information Technology, Economic Restructuring, and the Urban-Regional Process.* Oxford and Cambridge, Mass.: Blackwell.

Dempster, Murray W., Byron D. Klaus, and Douglas Petersen, eds. 1999. *The Globalization of Pentecostalism: A Religion Made to Travel.* Oxford and Irvine, Calif.: Regnum Books International.

Hoare, Rupert. 2000. "Information, Identity and Hope: Reading Castells." *Crucible* (April–June.): 70–89.

Hutton, Will, and Anthony Giddens, eds. 2000. *On the Edge: Living with Global Capitalism.* London: Jonathan Cape. (Published as Global Capitalism.) New York: The New Press.

INURA. 1998. *Possible Urban Worlds: Urban Strategies at the End of the Twentieth Century.* Basel and Boston: Birkhäuser Verlag.

Sassen, Saskia. 2001. *Global City: New York, London, Tokyo.* 2d ed. Princeton N.J.: Princeton University Press.

Scott, Allen J. 2001. *Global-City Regions.* Oxford: Oxford University Press.

Chapter 4: Shaping Communities for the Urban Future

References

Amin, Ash, Doreen Massey, and Nigel Thrift. 2000. *Cities for the Many and Not the Few.* Bristol: Policy Press.

CITY. 1996. "Towards a Habitable Future—an Interview with Nicholas You." *CITY—Analysis of Urban Trends, Culture, Theory, Policy, Action* 3 (4 June): 83–110.

Dussel, Enrique. 1988. *Ethics and Community*. Tunbridge Wells: Burns and Oates; Maryknoll, N.Y.: Orbis.

Gutiérrez, Gustavo. 1980. "Liberation Praxis and Christian Faith." *Frontiers of Theology in Latin America*. Edited by Rosino Gibellini. London: SCM Press; Maryknoll, N.Y.: Orbis.

Habitat. 1996. *Habitat Agenda and Istanbul Declaration*. New York: United Nations Department of Public Information. Online: www.unhabitat.org.

Hall, Peter, and Ulrich Pfeiffer. 2000. *Urban Future 21: A Global Agenda for Twenty-First-Century Cities*. London and New York: E&FN Spon.

hooks, bell. 1990. *Yearning: Race, Gender, and Cultural Politics*. Boston: South End Press; London: Turnaround (1991).

Jacobs, Jane. M. 1996. *Edge of Empire: Postcolonialism and the City*. London and New York: Routledge.

Landry, Charles. 1996. *The Art of Regeneration: Urban Renewal through Cultural Activity*. Stroud: Comedia.

Marcuse, Peter. 1994. "Not Chaos, but Walls: Postmodernism and the Partitioned City." *Postmodern Cities and Space*. Edited by Sophie Watson and Katherine Gibson. Oxford and Cambridge, Mass.: Blackwell.

Sandercock, Leonie. 2000. "When Strangers Become Neighbors: Managing Cities of Difference." *Planning Theory and Practice* 1, no. 1: 13–30. London: Routledge. Online: www .ar.utexas.edu/students/cadlab/wilson/Sandercock.html.

———. 1998a. "The Death of Modernist Planning: Radical Praxis for a Postmodern Age." *Cities for Citizens: Planning and the Rise of Civil Society in a Global Age*. Edited by Mike Douglass and John Friedmann. Chichester and New York: John Wiley & Sons.

———. 1998b. *Towards Cosmopolis—Planning for Multicultural Cities*. Chichester and New York: John Wiley & Sons.

Skinner, Steve. 1997. *Building Community Strengths—A Resource Book on Capacity Building.* London: Community Development Foundation Publications.

Soja, Edward. 1996. *Thirdspace: Journeys to Los Angeles and Other Real-and-Imagined Places.* Oxford and Malden, Mass.: Blackwell.

Stivers, Robert. 1976. *The Sustainable Society: Ethics and Economic Growth.* Philadelphia: Westminster. Extracted in *The Scope of Political Theology.* Edited by Alistair Kee. London: SCM Press (1978).

UNHCS. 2001. *Cities in a Globalizing World: Global Report on Human Settlements.* London: Earthscan.

United Nations. 1996. *An Urbanizing World. Global Report on Human Settlements 1996.* Oxford: Oxford University Press.

Further Reading

Beall, Jo, ed. 1997. *A City for All—Valuing Difference and Working with Diversity.* London and Atlantic Highlands, N.J.: Zed Books.

Fodor, Eben. 1999. *Better, Not Bigger: How to Take Control of Urban Growth and Improve Your Community.* Stony Creek, Conn.: New Society Publishers.

Gilbert, Alan, and Josef Gugler. 1994. *Cities, Poverty, and Development—Urbanization in the Third World.* Oxford: Oxford University Press.

Gratz, Roberta Brandes, and Norman Mintz. 1998. *Cities Back from the Edge: New Life for Downtown.* Chichester and New York: John Wiley & Sons.

Roussopoulos, Dimitrious. 2000. *Public Place: Citizen Participation in Neighborhood and Cities.* Toronto: Black Rose.

Sandercock, Leonie, ed. 1998. *Making the Invisible Visible: A Multicultural Planning History.* Berkeley: University of California Press.

UNHCS. 2001. *The State of the World's Cities Report 2001.* Nairobi: UNHCS.

Chapter 5: Reimaging the Biblical City

References

Brueggemann, Walter. 1977. *The Land—Place as Gift, Promise, and Challenge in Biblical Faith*. London: SPCK; Philadelphia: Fortress.

Day, Peggy L. 1995. "The Personification of Cities as Female in the Hebrew Bible: The Thesis of Aloysius Fitzgerald, FSC." *Social Location and Biblical Interpretation in Global Perspective*. Vol. 2 of *Reading from This Place*. Edited by Fernando F. Segovia and Mary Ann Tolbert. Minneapolis: Fortress.

Greenspoon, Leonard J. 2002. *"A Land Flowing with Milk and Honey": Visions of Israel from Biblical to Modern Times*. Omaha, Neb.: Creighton University Press.

Jacobs, Jane M. 1970. *The Economy of Cities*. London: Jonathan Cape; New York: Random House (1969).

Lee, Bernard J. 1995. *The Future Church of 140 B.C.E.: A Hidden Revolution*. New York: Crossroad Herder.

Limberg, James. 1993. *Jonah: A Commentary*. London: SCM Press.

Pixley, Jorge. 1992. *Biblical Israel: A People's History*. Minneapolis: Fortress.

Smith, Morton. 1987. *Palestinian Parties and Politics That Shaped the Old Testament*. London: SCM Press; New York: Columbia University Press (1971).

Soja, Edward. 2000. *Postmetropolis: Critical Studies of Cities and Regions*. Oxford and Malden, Mass.: Blackwell.

Van De Mieroop, Marc. 1997. *The Ancient Mesopotamian City*. Oxford: Clarendon.

VanGemeren, Willem A., ed. 1997. *New International Dictionary of Old Testament Theology and Exegesis*. Vol. 3. Carlisle: Paternoster; Grand Rapids, Mich.: Zondervan.

Further Reading

Brown, William P., and John T. Carroll. 2000. "The Garden and the Plaza: Biblical Images of the City." *Interpretation: A Journal of Bible and Theology* 5, no. 1: 3–11.

Fritz, Volkmar. 1994. *The City in Ancient Israel*. Sheffield: Sheffield Academic Press.

Gottwald, Norman K., and Richard A. Horsley, eds. 1993. *The Bible and Liberation: Political and Social Hermeneutics*. Rev. ed. London: SPCK; Maryknoll, N.Y.: Orbis.

Hawkins, Peter S., ed. 1986. *Civitas: Religious Interpretations of the City*. Atlanta: Scholars Press.

Chapter 6: Jesus: An Encounter with Urban Galilee and Jerusalem

References

Brueggemann, Walter. 1977. *The Land—Place as Gift, Promise, and Challenge in Biblical Faith*. London: SPCK; Philadelphia: Fortress.

Crossan, John Dominic. 1994. *Jesus: A Revolutionary Biography*. New York: HarperCollins.

———. 1998. *The Birth of Christianity*. Edinburgh: T&T Clark; San Francisco: HarperSanFrancisco (1999).

Freyne, Sean. 1995. "Herodian Economics in Galilee: Searching for a Suitable Model." *Modelling Early Christianity: Social–Scientific Studies of the New Testament in Its Context*. Edited by Philip F. Esler. London and New York: Routledge.

Herzog, William R., III. 2000. *Jesus, Justice, and the Reign of God: A Ministry of Liberation*. Louisville, Ky.: Westminster John Knox.

Myers, Ched. 1988. *Binding the Strong Man: A Political Reading of Mark's Story of Jesus*. Maryknoll, N.Y.: Orbis.

Reed, Jonathan. 2000. *Archaeology and the Galilean Jesus: A Reexamination of the Evidence*. Harrisburg, Pa.: Trinity Press International.

Rousseau, John J., and Rami Arav. 1996. *Jesus and His World: An Archaeological and Cultural Dictionary*. London: SCM Press; Minneapolis: Fortress.

Rowland, Christopher. 1993. "Reflections on the Politics of the Gospel." *The Kingdom of God and Human Society.* Edited by R. S. Barbour. Edinburgh: T&T Clark.

Sanders, E. P. 1993. *The Historical Figure of Jesus.* London and New York: Allen Lane—Penguin.

Sawicki, Marianne. 1994. *Seeing the Lord: Resurrection and Early Christian Practices.* Minneapolis: Fortress.

———. 2000. *Crossing Galilee: Architectures of Contact in the Occupied Land of Jesus.* Harrisburg, Pa.: Trinity Press International.

Wallace-Hadrill, Andrew. 1992. "Elites and Trade in the Roman Town." *City and Country in the Ancient World.* Edited by John Rich and Andrew Wallace-Hadrill. London and New York: Routledge.

Further Reading

Batey, Richard. 1991. *Jesus and the Forgotten City: New Light on Sepphoris and the Urban World of Jesus.* Grand Rapids, Mich.: Baker.

Crossan, John Dominic, and Jonathan L. Reed. 2001. *Excavating Jesus: Beneath the Stones, Behind the Text.* London: SPCK; San Francisco: HarperSanFrancisco.

Herzog, William R., III. 1994. *Parables as Subversive Speech: Jesus as Pedagogue of the Oppressed.* Louisville, Ky.: Westminster John Knox.

Horsley, Richard A. 1996. *Archaeology, History, and Society in Galilee.* Harrisburg, Pa.: Trinity Press International.

Theissen, Gerd, and Annette Merz. 1998. *The Historical Jesus: A Comprehensive Guide.* London: SCM Press; Minneapolis: Fortress.

Chapter 7: Retelling and Living the Story of Jesus in an Urban World

References

Achtemeier, Paul. 1985. *Romans.* Interpretation: A Bible Commentary for Teaching and Preaching. Louisville, Ky.: John Knox.

Barton, Stephen C. 1987. "Paul, Religion and Society." *Disciplines of Faith: Studies in Religion, Politics, and Patriarchy.* Edited by Jim Obelkevich, Lyndal Roper, and Raphael Samuel. London: RKP.

Bauckham, Richard. 1991. "Economic Critique of Rome in Revelation 18." *Images of Empire.* Edited by Alexander Loveday. Sheffield: JSOT Press.

Beavis, Mary Ann. 1997. " 'Expecting Nothing in Return': Luke's Picture of the Marginalized." *Gospel Interpretation: Narrative—Critical and Social Scientific Approaches.* Edited by Jack Dean Kingsbury. Harrisburg, Pa.: Trinity Press International.

Boff, Leonardo. 1985. *Church: Charism and Power.* London: SCM Press; Maryknoll, N.Y.: Orbis.

Boring, M. Eugene. 1989. *Revelation.* Interpretation: A Bible Commentary for Teaching and Preaching. Louisville, Ky.: John Knox.

Brueggemann, Walter. 1982. *Genesis.* Interpretation: A Bible Commentary for Preaching and Teaching. Louisville, Ky.: John Knox.

Clévenot, Michel. 1985. *Materialist Approaches to the Bible.* Maryknoll, N.Y.: Orbis.

Crosby, Michael. 1988. *House of Disciples: Church, Economics, and Justice in Matthew.* Maryknoll, N.Y.: Orbis.

Jewett, Robert. 1994. *Paul, The Apostle to America: Cultural Trends and Pauline Scholarship.* Louisville, Ky.: Westminster John Knox.

Meeks, Wayne A. 1983. *The First Urban Christians: The Social World of the Apostle Paul.* London and New Haven, Conn.: Yale University Press.

———. 1987. *Moral World of the First Christians.* London: SPCK; Philadelphia: Westminster.

Moxnes, Halvor. 1997. "The Social Context of Luke's Community." *Gospel Interpretation: Narrative—Critical and Social Scientific Approaches.* Edited by Jack Dean Kingsbury. Harrisburg, Pa.: Trinity Press International.

Murphy-O'Connor, Jerome. 1983. *St Paul's Corinth, Texts and Archaeology*. Collegeville, Minn.: Liturgical Press.

Rosing, Barbara R. 1999. *The Choice between Two Cities: Whore, Bride, and Empire*. Harrisburg, Pa.: Trinity Press International.

Rostagno, Sergio. n.d. *Essays on the New Testament—A "Materialist" Approach*. Geneva: WSCF.

Royalty, Robert R. 1998. *The Streets of Heaven: Ideology of Wealth in the Apocalypse of John*. Macon, Ga.: Mercer University Press.

Sandercock, Leonie, ed. 1998. *Making the Invisible Visible: A Multicultural Planning History*. Berkeley: University of California Press.

Sawicki, Marianne. 2000. *Crossing Galilee: Architectures of Contact in the Occupied Land of Jesus*. Harrisburg, Pa.: Trinity Press International.

Sykes, Stephen. 1995. *Unashamed Anglicanism*. London: Darton, Longman & Todd; Atlanta: Dimensions for Living.

Theissen, Gerd. 1983. *The Social Setting of Pauline Christianity: Essays on Corinth*. Edinburgh: T&T Clark; Philadelphia: Fortress.

Thompson, Leonard. 1990. *The Book of Revelation: Apocalypse and Empire*. Oxford and New York: Oxford University Press.

Young, Frances, and David Ford. 1988. *Meaning and Truth in 2 Corinthians*. London: SPCK.

Further Reading

Barton, Stephen C. 1997. "Christian Community in the Light of 1 Corinthians." *Studies in Christian Ethics* 10, no. 1: 1–15.

Corley, Kathleen. 1993. *Private Women, Public Meals: Social Conflict in the Synoptic Tradition*. Peabody, Mass.: Hendrickson.

Meggitt, Justin J. 1998. *Paul, Poverty, and Survival*. Edinburgh: T&T Clark.

Theissen, Gerd. 1999. *A Theory of Primitive Christian Religion*. London: SCM Press. Published as *The Religion of* the Earliest Churches: Creating a Symbolic World. Minneapolis: Fortress.

Chapter 8: Being Church—Between Local and Global

References

Amin, Ash, Doreen Massey, and Nigel Thrift. 2000. *Cities for the Many and Not the Few*. Bristol: Policy Press.

Aston Charities Trust. 1999. *Newham Directory of Religious Groups*. London: ACT. (Available from Durning Hall, Earlham Grove, London E7 9AB.)

Beckford, Robert. 1998. *Jesus Is Dread—Black Theology and Culture in Britain*. London: Darton, Longman & Todd.

———. 2000. *Dread and Pentecostal—A Political Theology for the Black Church in Britain*. London: SPCK.

———. 2001. *God of the Rahtid: Redeeming Rage*. London: Darton, Longman & Todd.

Budde, Michael L., and Robert W. Brimlow, eds. 2000. *The Church as Counterculture*. Albany N.Y.: State University of New York Press.

Carnes, Tony, and Anna Karpathakis, eds. 2001. *New York Glory: Religions in the City*. London and New York: New York University Press.

Chartres, Richard. 1995. "Church Ministry in London." *Church for the City*. Edited by Eric Blakebrough. London: Darton, Longman & Todd.

Chávez Sauceda, Teresa. 1996. "Becoming a Mestizo Church." *¡Alabadle! Hispanic Christian Worship*. Edited by Justo L. González. Nashville: Abingdon.

Davey, Andrew P. 1995. "Being Church as Political Praxis." *Liberation Theology UK*. Edited by Chris Rowland and John J. Vincent. Sheffield: Urban Theology Unit.

Davie, Grace. 1994. *Religion in Britain since 1945: Believing without Belonging*. Oxford and Cambridge, Mass.: Blackwell.

Dixon, Lorraine. 2000. "A Reflection on Black Identity and Belonging in the Context of the Anglican Church in England: A Way Forward." *Black Theology in Britain: A Journal of Contextual Praxis* 4: 22–37.

Edwards, Joel, ed. 1992. *"Let's Praise Him Again!" An African-Caribbean Perspective on Worship.* Eastbourne: Kingsway.

Evans, James H., Jr. 1985. "The Struggle for Identity: Black People in the Church of England." *Inheritors Together.* Edited by John L. Wilkinson, Renate Wilkinson, and James H. Evans Jr. London: General Synod Board for Social Responsibility.

Faramelli, Norman, Edward Rodman, and Anne Scheibner. 1996. "Seeking to Hear and to Heed in the Cities: Urban Ministry in the Postwar Episcopal Church." *Churches, Cities, and Human Community: Urban Ministry in the United States 1945–1985.* Edited by Clifford J. Green. Grand Rapids, Mich.: Eerdmans.

Giddens, Anthony. 1979. *Central Problems in Social Theory: Action, Structure, and Contradiction in Social Analysis.* London: Macmillan; Berkeley: University of California Press.

———. 1994. *New Rules of Sociological Method.* 2d ed. Cambridge: Polity Press; Stanford, Calif.: Stanford University Press.

Hari, Johann. 2001. "Barbarians Build the Barricades." *New Statesman*, 3 December, 28–29.

Hastings, Adrian. 2001. *A History of English Christianity 1920–2000.* 4th ed. London: SCM Press.

Lash, Nicholas. 1986. *Theology on the Road to Emmaus.* London: SCM Press.

Leech, Kenneth. 1988. *Struggle in Babylon: Racism and the Churches in Britain.* London: Sheldon Press.

Leong, Sze Tsung. 2001. "The Divine Economy." *Harvard Design School: Guide to Shopping.* Edited by Chuihua Judy Chung et al. Cambridge, Mass.: Harvard Design School.

Macpherson, William. 1999. *The Stephen Lawrence Inquiry: Report of an Inquiry by Sir William Macpherson of Cluny.* London: The Stationery Office.

Marcuse, Peter. 2000. "Cities in Quarters." *A Companion to the City.* Edited by Gary Bridge and Sophie Watson. Oxford and Malden Mass.: Blackwell.

Modood, Tariq, et al. 1997. *Ethnic Minorities in Britain: Diversity and Disadvantage. The Fourth National Survey of Ethnic Minorities.* London: Policy Studies Institute.

Putnam, Robert. 2000. *Bowling Alone: The Collapse and Revival of American Community.* New York: Simon & Schuster.

Sawicki, Marianne. 2000. "Salt and Leaven: Resistance to Empire in the Street-Smart Paleochurch." *The Church as Counterculture.* Edited by Michael L. Budde and Robert W. Brimlow. Albany, N.Y.: State University of New York Press.

Schillebeeckx, Edward. 1990. *Church: The Human Story of God.* London: SCM Press; New York: Crossroad.

Schreiter, Robert. 1997. *The New Catholicity: Theology between the Global and the Local.* Maryknoll. N.Y.: Orbis.

Smith, Greg. 1996. "The Unsecular City: The Revival of Religion in East London." *Rising in the East? The Regeneration of East London.* Edited by Tim Butler and Michael Rustin. London: Lawrence & Wishart.

Villafañe, Eldin. 1995. *Seek the Peace of the City—Reflections on Urban Ministry.* Grand Rapids, Mich.: Eerdmans.

Wilkinson, John. 1994. *The Church in Black and White.* Edinburgh: St. Andrew's Press.

Further Reading

Davey, Andrew P. 1998. "An Urban Way of Being Church: The Pastoral and Theological Dynamics of an Urban Church." Unpublished doctoral thesis. University of Sheffield.

Haslam, David. 1996. *Race for the Millennium.* London: CHP.

Parekh, Lord. 2000. *The Future of Multiethnic Britain.* London: Profile Books.

Chapter 9: Being Church—Between Presence and Flows

References

Boff, Leonardo. 1985. *Church: Charism and Power.* London: SCM Press; Maryknoll, N.Y.: Orbis.

Cavanaugh, William T. 2000. "The World in a Wafer: A Geography of the Eucharist as Resistance to Globalization." *Catholicism and Catholicity: Eucharistic Communities in Historical and Contemporary Perspectives.* Edited by Sarah Beckwith. Oxford and Malden, Mass.: Blackwell.

Crosby, Michael. 1988. *House of Disciples: Church, Economics, and Justice in Matthew.* Maryknoll, N.Y.: Orbis.

Ford, David. 1989. "Faith in the Cities: Corinth and the Modern City." *On Being the Church.* Edited by Colin Gunton and Daniel Hardy. Edinburgh: T&T Clark.

Ford, David, and Alistair McFadyen. 1995. *God in the City— Essays and Reflections from the Archbishop of Canterbury's Urban Theology Group.* Edited by Peter Sedgwick. London: Mowbray.

Kittel, Gerhard, and Gerhard Friedrich. 1985. *Theological Dictionary of the New Testament.* Translated and abridged by Geoffrey Bromiley. Exeter: Paternoster; Grand Rapids, Mich.: Eerdmans.

Moltmann, Jürgen. 1977. *The Church in the Power of the Spirit.* London: SCM Press; New York: Harper & Row.

Schreiter, Robert. 1997. *The New Catholicity: Theology between the Global and the Local.* Maryknoll, N.Y.: Orbis.

Schüssler Fiorenza, Elisabeth. 1983. *In Memory of Her: A Feminist Theological Reconstruction of Christian Origins.* London: SCM Press; New York: Crossroad.

Shanks, Norman. 1995. "Mission and Urbanization." *Theology in Scotland.* Edinburgh: University of St. Andrews.

Sheldrake, Philip. 2000. *Spaces for the Sacred: Place, Memory, Identity.* London: SCM Press.

Sobrino, Jon. 1985. *The True Church and the Poor.* London: SCM Press; Maryknoll, N.Y.: Orbis.

Sykes, Stephen. 1995. *Unashamed Anglicanism.* London: Darton, Longman & Todd; Atlanta: Dimensions for Living.

Young, Frances, and David Ford. 1988. *Meaning and Truth in 2 Corinthians.* London: SPCK.

Chapter 10: Being Church—Engaging and Connecting

References

Bundell, Kevan. 1999. *Local Lives and Livelihoods in a Global Economy.* London: Christian Aid.

Carnelley, Elizabeth. 1998. "Prophecy, Race, and Eastenders: Ministry on the Isle of Dogs and Celebrating the Difference." Extracted in *Urban Theology: A Reader.* Edited by Michael Northcott. London and Herndon, Va.: Cassell.

Castells, Manuel. 1989. *The Informational City: Information Technology, Economic Restructuring, and the Urban-Regional Process.* Oxford and Cambridge, Mass.: Blackwell.

———. 1997. *The Power of Identity.* Vol. 2 of *The Information Age: Economy, Society, and Culture.* Oxford and Malden, Mass.: Blackwell.

Dyson, David. 1999. "Lafayette Avenue Presbyterian Church." *Urban Churches, Vital Signs: Beyond Charity, Toward Justice.* Edited by Nile Harper. Grand Rapids, Mich.: Eerdmans.

Foster, Janet 1999. *Docklands: Cultures in Conflict: Worlds in Collision.* London: UCL Press.

Gillett, Richard. 2002. "Religion and Labor: Renewing the Alliance in Los Angeles." *Crucible* (January-March): 32–38.

Holtam, Nicholas, and Sue Mayo. 1998. *Learning from the Conflict: Reflections on the Struggle against the British National Party on the Isle of Dogs.* Jubilee Group. (Available from Jubilee Group, PO Box 356, Croydon CR9 7DS, UK.)

Safier, Michael. 1993. "Leading from the Ground Up: Institutional Landscapes, Institutional Innovations and the

Shifting Terms of Trade in Community-Led Urban Regeneration." *Regenerating Cities* 3–4 (March): 33–35.

Sassen, Saskia. 2000. "The Global City: Strategic Site/ New Frontier." *Democracy, Citizenship, and the Global City.* Edited by Engin F. Isin. London and New York: Routledge.

———. 2001. *The Global City: New York, London, Tokyo.* 2d ed. Princeton, N.J.: Princeton University Press.

Schreiter, Robert. 1997. *The New Catholicity: Theology between the Global and the Local.* Maryknoll, N.Y.: Orbis.

Shorter, Aylward. 1991. *The Church in the African City.* London: Geoffrey Chapman; Maryknoll, N.Y.: Orbis.

Valle, Victor, and Rodolfo Torres. 2000. *Latino Metropolis.* Minneapolis and London: University of Minnesota Press.

Wylie Kellerman, Bill. 1996. "Resisting Death Incarnate— The Principalities of Urban Violence." *Sojourners* (April): 160.

Further Reading

Bartlett, Sheridan, and David Satterthwaite. 2000. *Cities for Children: Children's Rights, Poverty, and Urban Management.* London: Earthscan.

Carle, Robert D., and Louis A. Decaro. 1997. *Signs of Hope in the City: Ministries of Community Renewal.* Valley Forge, Pa.: Judson.

Eade, John, ed. 1997. *Living the Global City—Globalization as Local Process.* London and New York: Routledge.

Green, Laurie. 2000. *The Impact of the Global: An Urban Theology.* Sheffield: Urban Theology Unit.

Recinos, Harold J. 1992. *Jesus Weeps: Global Encounters on Our Doorstep.* Nashville: Abingdon.

Rumschiedt, Barbara. 1999. *No Room for Grace: Pastoral Theology and Dehumanization in the Global Economy.* Grand Rapids, Mich.: Eerdmans.

Russell, Hilary. 1995. *Poverty Close to Home—A Christian Understanding.* London: Mowbrays.

Stackhouse, Max, Tim Dearborn, and Scott Paeth. 2000. *The Local Church in a Global Era: Reflections for a New Century.* Grand Rapids, Mich.: Eerdmans.

Chapter 11: Faith in the Fugure of an Urbanizing World

References

Castells, Manuel. 1989. *The Informational City: Information Technology, Economic Restructuring, and the Urban-Regional Process.* Oxford and Cambridge, Mass.: Blackwell.

Davis, Mike. 1992. *City of Quartz: Excavating the Future in Los Angeles.* New York: Vintage; London: Pimlico (1998).

de Certeau, Michel. 1984. *The Practice of Everyday Life.* Berkeley: University of California Press.

Gibson, William. 1984. *Neuromancer.* London: Gollancz; New York: Ace.

————. 1994. *Virtual Light.* New York: Viking/Bantam.

————. 1996. *Idoru.* London: Viking; New York: Putnam.

————. 1999. *All Tomorrow's Parties.* London: Viking; New York: Putnam.

Harvey, David. 2000. *Spaces of Hope.* Edinburgh: Edinburgh University Press.

Marcuse, Peter. 1994. "Not Chaos, but Walls: Postmodernism and the Partitioned City." *Postmodern Cities and Space.* Edited by Sophie Watson and Katherine Gibson. Oxford and Cambridge, Mass.: Blackwell.

————. 2001. "Reflections on the Events: Urban Life Will Change." *CITY—Analysis of Urban Trends, Culture, Theory, Policy, Action* 5, no. 3: 394–97.

Mendieta, Eduardo. 2001. "The Space of Terror, the Utopian City: On the Attack on the World Trade Center." *CITY—Analysis of Urban Trends, Culture, Theory, Policy, Action* 5, no. 3: 397–406.

Safier, Michael. 2001. "Confronting 'Urbicide': Crimes against Humanity, Civility, and Diversity and the Case for a Civic Cosmopolitan Response to the Attack on New York City."

CITY—*Analysis of Urban Trends, Culture, Theory, Policy, Action* 5, no. 3: 416–29.

Sandercock, Leonie. 1998. *Towards Cosmopolis—Planning for Multicultural Cities.* Chichester and New York: John Wiley & Sons.

Williams, Rowan. 2002. *Writing in the Dust: Reflections on 11th September and Its Aftermath.* London: Hodder & Stoughton; Grand Rapids, Mich.: Eerdmans.

Wink, Walter. 1998. *The Powers That Be.* New York: Doubleday.

Index of Modern Authors

Index of Subjects